Teaching in the
New Kindergarten

Join us on the web at
EarlyChildEd.delmar.com

Teaching in the New Kindergarten

J. Amos Hatch
University of Tennessee

THOMSON

DELMAR LEARNING

Australia Canada Mexico Singapore Spain United Kingdom United States

THOMSON

DELMAR LEARNING

Teaching in the New Kindergarten
J. Amos Hatch

Vice President,
Career Education SBU:
Dawn Gerrain

Director of Editorial:
Sherry Gomoll

Acquisitions Editor:
Erin O'Connor

Editorial Assistant:
Ivy Ip

Director of Production:
Wendy A. Troeger

Production Editor:
Joy Kocsis

Technology Project Manager:
Joseph Saba

Director of Marketing:
Wendy E. Mapstone

Channel Manager:
Donna J. Lewis

Cover Design:
Joseph Villanova

Composition:
Pre-Press Company, Inc.

Cover Image:
© Getty Images

NOTICE TO THE READER

Publisher does not warrant or guarantee any of the products described herein or perform any independent analysis in connection with any of the product information contained herein. Publisher does not assume, and expressly disclaims, any obligation to obtain and include information other than that provided to it by the manufacturer.

The reader is expressly warned to consider and adopt all safety precautions that might be indicated by the activities herein and to avoid all potential hazards. By following the instructions contained herein, the reader willingly assumes all risks in connection with such instructions.

The Publisher makes no representation or warranties of any kind, including but not limited to, the warranties of fitness for particular purpose or merchantability, nor are any such representations implied with respect to the material set forth herein, and the publisher takes no responsibility with respect to such material. The publisher shall not be liable for any special, consequential, or exemplary damages resulting, in whole or part, from the readers' use of, or reliance upon, this material.

Contents

Preface vii

CHAPTER | 1

Why do we need a new kindergarten? 2

Changing experiences—children and families in the
    postmodern age 4

Changing understandings—Vygotsky and beyond 8

Changing expectations—kindergarten teaching and the standards
    movement 16

Closing thoughts 18

CHAPTER | 2

What do I teach in the new kindergarten? 24

Language arts 29

Mathematics 38

Science 46

Social studies 51

Health and physical education 57

Art and music 62

Closing thoughts 65

CHAPTER | 3

How do I teach in the new kindergarten? 68

Teacher as professional problem solver 70

A continuum of teaching strategies 74

Using the continuum—Examples of incidental, thematic, strategic,
    and direct teaching 99

Closing thoughts 107

CHAPTER | 4

How do I organize and manage a new kindergarten classroom?

How do I organize and manage a new kindergarten classroom? 110

Balancing rights and responsibilities—Everyone is responsible for accomplishing the purposes of the group 113

Balancing the arrangement of space—Every space has a purpose 116

Balancing the presentation of activities—Every task has a purpose 120

Balancing the organization of time—Every minute has a purpose 124

Balancing assessment—Learn a little every day and make a record of what was learned 129

Balancing differences in children's abilities—Including all children in the learning process 132

Balancing parent and community involvement—Reciprocal relations as a genuine goal 138

Keeping your balance—Dealing with threats to classroom equilibrium 142

Closing thoughts 149

CHAPTER | 5

What will a week look like in a new kindergarten classroom?

What will a week look like in a new kindergarten classroom? 152

Monday 153

Tuesday 159

Wednesday 164

Thursday 168

Friday 172

Closing thoughts 177

References 181

Preface

I have written this book for those who want to provide high-quality kindergarten experiences for children in the changing contexts of the twenty-first century. It is designed for students learning how to be teachers and for educators who want to improve the kindergarten programs for which they are responsible. The book assumes that new approaches to kindergarten teaching are needed to keep pace with rapid changes in the world, especially increasing academic expectations for young children. It is a systematic attempt to bring together a variety of perspectives in practical ways so that new teachers can organize and run successful kindergarten programs that meet the needs of individual children while providing experiences that take into account the influences of living in a postmodern world, reflect richer understandings of teaching and learning, and meet the expectations of those who would impose standards on teachers and children.

Kindergarten is changing. Kindergarten teachers are being pressured to accelerate the learning of their students, especially in the area of literacy. Many teachers prepared to teach in traditional early childhood programs are at a loss for what to do given the press of standards-based reform efforts at national, state, local, and school levels. Preservice teachers who anticipate starting their careers in contemporary kindergartens are not sure they will be able to provide programs that serve the needs of their students *and* satisfy the academic expectations of their supervisors. This is a book for kindergarten teachers and teachers in training that provides ways for them to meet the demands of outside forces and be true to their commitment to young children.

In *Teaching in the New Kindergarten*, I redefine kindergarten teaching by challenging the dichotomous thinking that characterizes most approaches (e.g., either you have a developmentally appropriate or an academic program; either you are a whole language or a phonics teacher). In place of the either/or discourse that dominates discussions of appropriate kindergarten teaching, I offer a balanced approach that goes beyond simple compromises. I advocate processing complex information from a variety of sources and applying that information to the particulars of individual communities, schools, and classrooms. Teachers are treated as professional decision makers, and models for making sound decisions are described in detail throughout the book.

I have organized this book so that new teachers can build a solid foundation for creating and operating an effective kindergarten program. The language and tone are personal and practical. I write in first person, use plenty of real-world examples, and frame the discussion in terms that are familiar to preservice teachers. The first chapter establishes the need for a new kindergarten and describes the elements that make the approach taken in the book unique. The second chapter describes a complete curriculum for the new kindergarten, organizing content across curriculum domains and explaining each curriculum element in straightforward, accessible language. Chapter 3 describes a continuum of teaching strategies from incidental to direct teaching and gives specific examples of how each teaching strategy can be applied to specific content from the curriculum described in Chapter 2. The fourth chapter describes ways to organize and manage new kindergarten classrooms based on the idea that learning ought to be taken seriously as the purpose of schooling. The final chapter is a detailed description of one week's instruction that provides a comprehensive example of how the ideas in the book might play out in a real classroom.

The book has several elements that make it a valuable primary source for new kindergarten teachers. Distinguishing features include:

- an introductory chapter explaining why we need a new kindergarten and giving teachers a reason and permission to do a program that includes real, systematic learning that addresses standards imposed by others, while meeting the needs of the child

- the presentation of a complete kindergarten curriculum so teachers will not have to guess what to teach in each of the subject matter areas

- a chapter on instruction that breaks down the barriers between developmental and academic approaches, providing teachers with balanced, explicit means to help children succeed academically while providing appropriate instruction

- a chapter on organizing and managing kindergarten classrooms, giving new teachers detailed suggestions for making learning the centerpiece of daily activity and dealing with forces that can keep that from happening

- a comprehensive description of one week's classroom activities that shows teachers how curriculum, instruction, and management practices blend together

- a detailed problem-solving model for teachers and specific examples of its application to genuine classroom problems

- a sample daily schedule and an example of its implementation through the eyes of a kindergarten student

- a section demonstrating ways to link specific elements of curriculum content with a variety of teaching strategies

- a detailed example of ways to adjust when children do not buy into the recommended classroom management approach

- the presentation of several examples that demonstrate the thinking behind creating modifications for children with disabilities

- a broad theoretical and research base that takes the consideration of appropriate practices beyond the usual polarized conflict between constructivist and behaviorist approaches

- the presentation of key terms and concepts at the beginning of each chapter to serve as and advance organizer that lets readers know the most important elements to be covered in the chapter

- the inclusion of learning activities (for individuals, small groups, and large groups) at the conclusion of each chapter to provide teachers, students, and instructors with ideas for actively applying ideas in the chapter

- the provision of a "For Your Consideration" section at the close of each chapter that presents higher-order questions designed to encourage readers to thoughtfully consider issues raised by chapter contents

- the integration of application activities throughout the book that take quotes from the text and ask readers to consider direct applications of the ideas in the quotes to real kindergarten contexts.

Online Companion™

The Online Companion™ to accompany *Teaching in the New Kindergarten* is your link to early childhood education on the Internet. The Online Companion™ contains downloadable/printable versions of the following features found in the text which you can print easily for reference:

- Applications

- For Your Consideration

- Learning Activities

 The Online Companion™ icon appears next to features in the text which will also appear on-line.

You can find the Online Companion™ at www.earlychilded.delmar.com

The author would like to thank the following reviewers, enlisted by Thomson Delmar Learning, for their helpful suggestions and constructive criticism:

Kim Ann Bozenhardt, Ed D
Dauphin Way Child Development Center
Moblie, AL

Karen Danbom, PhD
Minnesota State University
Moorhead, MN

Stacey Dudley
Bowing Green State University
Bowling Green, OH

Judy Lindman
Rochester Community and Technical College
Rochester, MN

Carol Marxen
Universtiy of Minnesota, Morris
Morris, MN

Judy Rose-Paterson
Pilgrim's Children's Center
Carlsbad, CA

Gloria Transits-Wenze, PhD
University of Scranton
Scranton, PA

Dedication

To all the kindergarten teachers who have helped me understand what it means to do this incredible work, especially Margaret, Lou Ann, Becky, Emily, Pam, Donna, Shari, Patricia, Debbie, and Ginger.

CHAPTER | 1

Why Do We Need a New Kindergarten?

KEY TERMS AND CONCEPTS

Postmodern childhood

• Permeable versus nuclear families

• Modern versus postmodern values

• Hurried children

Theoretical camps

• Maturationism

• Behaviorism

• Constructivism

Balanced approach

Reggio Emilia

Project Spectrum

• Multiple intelligences

• Nonuniversal theory

Reading research syntheses

Intentional learning

Postmodern critique

• Grand narratives

• Multiple truths

Standards-based reform

Accountability shovedown

There's nothing new under the sun. I believe this old axiom, but I also believe that the world is being reinvented every day. Certainly, the social context in which kindergarten teachers operate has undergone dramatic change over the past several years. The experience of being a child in contemporary culture is vastly different from what it was just a generation ago. Knowledge about how children learn and develop has exploded. Powerful forces are competing over what children ought to learn in kindergarten, how they should be taught, and how they ought to be assessed. These changes and others mean that traditional ways of doing kindergarten may no longer be the best ways. It's time for a new kindergarten that takes the best of traditional approaches, integrates emerg-

The experience of childhood today is different from what it was even a generation ago.

ing understandings of what young children are like and what they need, and meets the challenge of the accountability movement being pushed down into early childhood education. This book describes a kindergarten that is new in the sense that it directly addresses the needs of five- and six-year-old children who live in a world that is being reinvented more rapidly than at any time in history.

This chapter is designed to give you several reasons for paying attention to the rest of this book and lays out the framework that holds the book's ideas together. I argue that rapid changes in the world have direct implications for how kindergarten programs ought to be organized and how kindergartners ought to be taught. Three specific areas of dramatic change are addressed head-on: changing experiences (it is clear that the experience of childhood today is different from what it was even a generation ago); changing understandings (traditional perspectives on how children learn and develop have been challenged, altered, and enriched by new ways of thinking that have been slow to find their way into kindergarten curricula and teaching); and changing expectations (the press for standards-based reform poses an imminent challenge to kindergarten teachers that will not go away soon). Once a rationale is set out, I outline the distinguishing features of the new kindergarten.

My goal is for readers to be able to use this book as a framework for setting up and running kindergarten programs focused on meeting the needs of each child, while providing experiences that take into account the influences of living in a postmodern world. These programs should reflect richer understandings of teaching and learning, while addressing the expectations of the accountability movement on teachers and children. My approach is not to take a defensive stance in relation to rapid change, but to rethink what constitutes good practice and organize classrooms and programs in ways that apply what we know about learning and teaching. This approach assumes that, first and foremost, we are teachers because we are committed to improving the life chances of children.

Changing Experiences— Children and Families in the Postmodern Age

My early childhood training taught me to believe that children are children— that certain characteristics define what a child is and that these characteristics are universal across cultures, settings, and time. I'm not as sure of this basic concept as I used to be. What I am sure of is that the experience of being a child is strongly affected by culture, place, and time. Being a child in Cameroon is very different from being a child in Canada; childhood in East St. Louis is markedly different from childhood in Scarsdale; and childhood today is significantly different from what it was even 10 years ago. While it's probably a good thing for kindergarten teachers to see the universal qualities that make their children children, operating kindergartens as if all children bring the same experiences, strengths, and needs to school is a mistake. I believe that providing kindergarten programs based on the assumption that five- and six-year-old children are pretty much the same as they were in the past is also a mistake. The world in which we live is changing at unprecedented speed, and everything we know suggests that change will only accelerate. The lifeworlds of young children have changed, and we need kindergarten programs that respond.

For starters, more young children experience out-of-home care than ever before, and they start receiving it at younger and younger ages. As economic conditions, societal values, and marital patterns have changed, more children are being raised by individuals who are not members of their nuclear families. I don't see this as an inherently good or bad thing, but the fact that so many children are placed in childcare settings earlier in their lives means that they will come to school with different backgrounds and needs from children a few generations ago, who predominantly came from situations in which they were cared for almost exclusively by their mothers until ready to start kindergarten.

In addition to the numbers of children served, the experiences provided in childcare and preschool settings have changed. In most communities, pre-school programs of all types have taken a much more academic focus over the past several years. Parents who place their children in preschools expect that their children will learn skills and content that would not have been taught a few generations ago. Government-subsidized preschool programs have increased their emphasis on giving an academic head start to children who are at risk of beginning school at a disadvantage in relation to their more affluent peers. Kindergarten programs that have not changed in response to these realities may not be providing experiences that meet the needs of the children they serve.

A related change in how being a child is different today is reflected in the organization of family life. As a society, the norms for families have been altered from a nuclear family structure to what David Elkind (1994) calls **permeable families.** The traditional **nuclear family** with a working dad and stay-at-home mom who shared the primary goal of making life better for their children has been replaced by the postmodern permeable family in which parental roles are blurred, individual autonomy is valued more highly than togetherness, and parents' needs often come before those of children. What this means for kindergarten teachers is that their students will be coming from families that vary greatly from traditional norms in terms of who is doing the parenting and what kind of parenting gets done. More children will experience divorce, more children will live in single-parent families, more children will live in dual-wage families, more children will experience foster care, more children will live in homes with same-sex parents, and more children will be raised by family members who are not their biological parents. My point is not that families used to be good and now they're bad. The point is that children entering school are coming with different backgrounds and values because they have been living in families that are put together and function differently from the traditional families that were assumed to exist when most current kindergarten programs were designed.

The pervasive influence of media has also changed the experience of growing up in our society. Television is the prime example. Young children watch television from infancy and spend larger portions of their time in front of the tube than doing any other waking activity. The sheer amount of time is a concern because that time is not used in ways that might be more beneficial to their learning and development, such as interacting with others, playing, or being physically active.

The content children watch is another major concern. Neil Postman (1982) argues that childhood is disappearing because adults have no secrets

Postmodern families function differently than the traditional families that were assumed to exist in the past.

from children. Knowledge that used to mark differences between generations is now broadcast around the clock on TV, and children are watching. Teachers know that adult language, adult sexual knowledge, and adult perspectives on violence are no longer taboo for many young children. Other popular media such as music, movies, video games, and the Internet contribute to a significant shift in the activity patterns, understandings, and values that kindergartners bring to school.

I believe the media both reflect and create changes in social values. The postmodern world in which children are growing up can be characterized by a variety of new social norms, and these **postmodern values** influence the learning and development of young children in significant ways. Some pertinent examples of postmodern norms include the following:

- Form and style are more important than content and substance.
- Self-identity is not stable, but changes according to the situation.
- Feelings have been separated from experience.
- Time is fragmented into a series of perpetual presents.
- Simulations of reality are valued over real experience (Hatch, 2000).

How these shifting values play out differs for different children in different families and communities, but the life experiences of all children are impacted. Even a quick look at the postmodern norms listed ought to give kindergarten teachers and program developers pause. For example, traditional bases for curriculum, instruction, and classroom management are challenged if we take seriously the ideas that style is more important than substance, that virtual reality is preferable to direct experience, and that self-identity is always temporary. My position is not that we should capitulate to changing social norms, but that we are just plain foolish if we ignore them.

Critics of this view may argue that every generation undergoes change. I agree with that basic concept, but it's evident to me that change is occurring more rapidly and is placing more stress on children than ever before. Contemporary children are expected to grow up fast. Not long ago, adults saw it as their obligation to guard the innocence of children, protecting them from the harsh realities of the world. Adults now expect children to develop the competence to handle their own problems (Elkind, 2001). Our basic approach has shifted from protecting children from stressors such as divorce, drugs, violence, and being left alone to providing coping skills for dealing with divorce, tools for saying no to drugs, strategies for reacting to and reporting violence, and skills for staying safe when no adults are present.

Elkind argues convincingly that shifting responsibility away from adults **hurries children** to grow up too fast too soon and causes them to experience stress at levels that can be harmful. This means that the children entering kindergarten may be more competent and less dependent on adults than children a generation ago; more self-reliant and less interested in adult guidance; and feeling more stress and less security. Again, the changing conditions and potential consequences described are not all good or all bad, but they do influence how children think and act in classroom settings.

The postmodern world in which young children are being raised creates environments and experiences that have changed the experience of being a child. Experiences with out-of-home care at an early age, lessons learned in changing family structures, the profound influence of the media, the changing values structure in our society, and increased pressure on children to grow up quickly all contribute to altering the experience of contemporary childhood. Outstanding teachers and instructional leaders have recognized the significance of these changes for kindergarten teaching and have made adjustments to traditional approaches, but these innovators are few and far between.

This book is about setting up curriculum, thinking about teaching, and developing classroom management strategies that address these changes while maintaining what is best about traditional programs. To imagine that such changes will go away is naive; to pretend that they do not significantly effect what happens in kindergarten is foolish. A new approach to kindergarten is needed.

Changing Understandings— Vygotsky and Beyond

The field of early childhood education is contested territory. Strong camps oppose each other on basic questions of how best to educate kindergartners. As recently as 15 years ago, it was possible to divide the contestants into three major factions: maturationists, behaviorists, and constructivists (Hatch & Freeman, 1988).

- The **maturationist** perspective, articulated by Gesell and others, stresses the role of genetically controlled biological change in behavior and learning. Kindergartens designed on maturationist principles are much like nursery schools where safe, nurturing environments are set up so children can develop naturally without systematic adult intervention.

- **Behaviorists,** such as Skinner and his followers, emphasize the importance of environmental factors on children's learning. Behaviorist kindergartens look like academic primary classrooms in which learning is broken down into manageable segments that adults teach using direct instruction and behavior modification techniques.

- **Constructivist** theory is based on the work of Piaget and his disciples, and assumes that development is a dynamic process that involves children in the construction of their own knowledge as a result of the interaction of biology and experience. Kindergartens that implement constructivist practices are designed in ways that encourage children to explore and discover, while adults set up environments and activities that support children's development.

In many ways, the history of kindergarten education in the twentieth century can be characterized by charting the rise and fall of these competing perspectives, with behaviorism and constructivism dominating over the past 30 years. But other ways of thinking about organizing and doing kindergarten have much to add to our understanding. It's popular to talk about taking a **balanced approach**

Scaffolding children's learning can accelerate their development.

to kindergarten teaching, which in the current context means picking the best of behaviorist and constructivist ideas. I like the idea of a balanced approach and use it throughout this book. However, the balance we need is not simply to add equal parts of two dominant perspectives but to create a balance among that which we have known for a long time and the many exciting sources of information that are becoming available as time goes on. Some of the sources that have influenced the design of what I call the new kindergarten follow.

The work of Lev Vygotsky (1962, 1978) is certainly not new; he completed it in the 1920s and early 1930s, and it came to be appreciated by early childhood educators late in the twentieth century. *Appreciated* is not the same as *applied*. The serious application of some of Vygotsky's basic principles would change how children are taught and assessed in kindergarten. For example, Vygotsky argued that children's development can be accelerated when they are challenged to work beyond their individual capacities and are supported by others competent in the skills or content they are trying to master. A systematic scaffolding process between learner and teacher recognizes the social dimension of all learning and provides tools for teaching children material that is just beyond what they can master on their own (Bedrova & Leong, 1996; Berk & Winsler, 1995).

APPLICATIONS

Knowledge is constructed in social interaction between children and more knowledgeable others.

Imagine that you are preparing for an upcoming parent night during which you will be describing your approach to kindergarten teaching to the parents of your students. As part of your orientation, you want to explain to parents the important role they play in helping their children learn and develop. Write out a plan for how you would teach parents the importance of scaffolding their children's learning. Provide concrete tips and use examples to demonstrate Vygotsky's notion that more knowledgeable others (in this case, parents) can help children do things with help that they could not do alone.

The constructivist and behaviorist approaches that have ruled the debate on best kindergarten practices prescribe opposite roles for the teacher:

- Constructivists see teachers as facilitators who set up environments in which children explore, discover, and construct their own knowledge.
- Behaviorist teachers use direct instruction techniques and reinforcement regimens to pass knowledge along in small bits.

Neither reflects Vygotsky's understanding that knowledge is constructed in social interaction between children and more knowledgeable others. Likewise, Vygotsky's notion that assessment ought to include figuring out what children can do with assistance (i.e., identifying the area in which instruction would be most effective) is widely known but seldom applied. The ideas may have been around for a while, but using what we have learned from Vygotsky and some of his followers (Rogoff, 1990; Wertsch, 1991) to rethink teaching and assessment in kindergarten would be new.

Another source of knowledge about good early childhood practice that has been sparingly applied in kindergarten settings is the **Reggio Emilia** approach, developed in Italy (Edwards, Gandini, & Forman, 1993). Reggio preschools actually apply some of Vygotsky's and Rogoff's ideas, as well as what Reggio educators have learned from other theorists and developed through their own reflective practices. While I am very cautious about translating understandings gained from preschool programs in a specific cultural context to kindergarten programs in general, I believe some of the lessons from Reggio do have importance for reshaping a new kindergarten. For example, in Reggio schools, chil-

Children can be full partners in the education process.

dren are seen as protagonists (they are strong, rich, capable, and full partners in the education process), collaborators (their learning happens in social relationships with other children, teachers, families, and community members), and communicators (they are capable of representing what they know using a variety of symbolic means) (Cadwell, 1997). These roles are not emphasized in kindergarten classrooms shaped by constructivist or behaviorist philosophies. I believe part of developing a new kindergarten is to rethink the roles of the student, and the Reggio approach offers insights into what is possible in this and other areas.

Project Spectrum is a program for preschool and early elementary students developed around the idea that children have a far wider range of abilities than is usually recognized or valued in school (Chen, Krechevsky, & Viens, 1998). The original project and the applications that followed are examples of what is possible when new ways of thinking about children's capacities are implemented. Based on Gardner's (1993, 1998) theory of **multiple intelligences** and Feldman's (1994) **nonuniversal theory,** Project Spectrum demonstrates the efficacy of developing curriculum and assessment strategies with a broadened perspective on the capacities of the human mind. Multiple intelligence and nonuniversal theories are based in cognitive psychology and provide important understandings that ought to influence how education happens in kindergarten classrooms. For example, an active recognition that kindergartners will exhibit a variety of intelligences (i.e., verbal, logical-mathematical, musical, spatial, bodily kinesthetic, intrapersonal, interpersonal, and naturalistic) will mean that learning activities will come in a variety of forms. Understanding principles of nonuniversal theory (e.g., that children have individual and cultural proclivities that often go unrecognized when traditional developmental perspectives are applied) will lead kindergarten teachers to create curriculum, instruction, and assessment practices that look different from those based on either constructivist or behaviorist constructs.

Other findings from cognitive researchers provide revealing insights into how children process information, remember it, and apply what they have learned. The Committee on Developments in the Science of Learning of the National Research Council synthesized research on human learning in *How People Learn* (Bransford, Brown, & Cocking, 1999). Their synthesis challenges traditional views of the developmental limitations attributed to young learners, and it highlights the importance of helping children acquire a variety of strategies for **intentional learning.** Children are capable of understanding learning processes and intentionally directing their own learning at levels we did not recognize when we designed early childhood programs in the past. The report argues that in order to develop strategic competence in learning, "children need to understand what it means to learn, who they are as learners, and how they go about planning, monitoring, revising, and reflecting on their own learn-

APPLICATIONS

Children are capable of understanding learning processes and intentionally directing their own learning.

Imagine that the other kindergarten teachers at your school are determined to maintain the classroom practices that they have used for years. One of their fundamental beliefs is that five- and six-year-olds are egocentric and incapable of metacognitive reflection (i.e., thinking about their own thinking). In your grade-level planning meetings, they challenge you to justify your emphasis on intentional learning processes. Think through how you might explain the efficacy of your approach without alienating your colleagues. Construct rational explanations in terms that they can understand, and think of examples that might help them see your case.

ing" (p. 100). These are worthy goals for an effective contemporary kindergarten program. Setting up programs that strengthen children's understandings of what learning is all about and how they operate as learners, including the development of metacognitive strategies for monitoring their own learning, should be emphasized in the new kindergarten.

Another important source of knowledge that ought to influence the new kindergarten is the recent flurry of **reading research syntheses** (e.g., National Reading Panel, 2000; NEA, 2000; Neuman, Copple, & Bredekamp, 2000; Snow, Burns, & Griffin, 1998). Attempting to resolve the great reading wars that have raged between behaviorist (phonics based) and constructivist (whole language) approaches, independent teams of scholars have examined the research evidence and identified guiding principles. For the most part, they have found that neither a behaviorist nor a constructivist approach by itself will provide all children with what they need to learn to read and write. Because the kindergarten experience is pivotal to children's literacy development, applying current understandings about teaching children to read and write is essential. For example, the reading reports indicate that children need to understand the alphabetic principle to become proficient readers; that phonemic awareness is one of the best predictors of success in reading; that systematic, but meaningful, code instruction produces significant benefits for children who have difficulties learning to read; that vocabulary should be taught directly and indirectly; and that daily reading to children builds interest in reading and knowledge of how proficient readers operate on books. These and other generalizations from current research on literacy learning deserve a prominent place in contemporary kindergarten curriculum.

APPLICATIONS

Systematic, but meaningful, code instruction produces significant benefits for children who have difficulties learning to read.

Imagine you are at a social event attended by individuals who are not professional educators. Some of the people you are talking with believe that children are not learning to read because schools are not teaching phonics. Construct an explanation of your approach to systematic code instruction, emphasizing the importance of *meaningful* phonics instruction, as opposed to excessive drill and rote practice of isolated phonics elements.

Teachers model how proficient readers operate on text.

A final area from which enriched perspectives on kindergarten can be gained is the new discipline of **postmodern critique.** I have argued that the experience of childhood is changing because children are growing up in a postmodern world. A new area of inquiry is showing us that notions of truth are changing because of postmodern perspectives on what counts as knowledge. Modern ideas such as the possibility of uncovering universal truths through the application of scientific principles are being replaced with the postmodern understanding that **multiple truths** exist and that these are always local, partial, and in flux (Hatch, 2000). Postmodern scholars interested in studying early childhood critique assumptions concerning development, learning, and teaching at the core of the field. They challenge the **grand narratives** (e.g., behaviorism, maturationism, constructivism) that experts in early childhood education use to justify making pronouncements about how best to teach young children and guide their development (Cannella & Bailey, 1999, p. 7).

What does this mean for kindergarten teachers and for a book about kindergarten teaching? For me, it means that teachers and others responsible

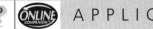 APPLICATIONS

Kindergarten educators should examine the "truth" of what is being proposed in relation to the special circumstances in which they work.

Imagine that you had absolute freedom to create a kindergarten program from scratch. What information about the special circumstances of your classroom, school, and community should you examine before you begin making decisions about curriculum, teaching, classroom organization, materials, and assessment? Make a list of questions that would generate the information you would need to make good decisions that take into account the unique characteristics of particular contexts.

for kindergarten education should take the curriculum, instruction, and assessment approaches they are encouraged (or required) to implement with a grain of salt. Whether it's a behaviorist program like direct instruction models (Becker, Engelmann, Carnine, & Rhine, 1981), a constructivist approach such as that embodied in developmentally appropriate practices (Bredekamp & Copple, 1997), or the balanced framework suggested in this book, kindergarten educators should examine the "truth" of what is being proposed in relation to the special circumstances in which they work. This book tries to provide a framework that assists teachers in making good decisions, but it is understood throughout that every setting, every class of children, and every teacher is unique. Recognizing that multiple ways of teaching and guiding children are not only possible, but essential, is a postmodern realization that is central to this book.

In this section, I have touched briefly on some of the understandings that I believe ought to influence how twenty-first century kindergarten programs are planned and implemented. While bits and pieces of these new understandings have found their way into some classrooms and some programs, I think they have been largely ignored. Schools are inherently conservative places where genuine change is slow. Traditional approaches will not go away, nor should they. But implementing alternative perspectives like those described would bring a much more complex balance to the teaching of kindergarten. This balance goes beyond finding what's best in skills-based and integrated teaching; it means taking a broad view of what's possible and working hard to create experiences that optimize children's learning in the new kindergarten.

Changing Expectations—
Kindergarten Teaching and the
Standards Movement

I have discussed changes in the social contexts of childhood and the theoretical and research contexts of early childhood knowledge. This section is about political change. I am convinced that political forces drive the standards movement that permeates education at all levels. It's hard for me to fathom how the logic of **standards-based reform** can be applied to the education of young children. I find the idea that kindergarten children and their teachers should be threatened with failure if they do not meet certain arbitrary standards to be disturbing. But the facts of life are that politicians, business leaders, and some educators are pushing accountability based on standards down to the kindergarten level and below—a phenomenon I call **accountability shovedown** (Hatch, 2002, p. 461). Expectations for improved kindergarten performance on specific academic skills are already in place or on their way (Dever, Falconer, & Kessenich, 2003; Hoff, 2002). These expectations are changing the ways kindergarten teachers think about and do their jobs. Calling for standards-based reform that includes our youngest learners makes political hay, and it will not go away.

Just because it's political does not make the consequences of implementing standards-based accountability measures in kindergarten any less real. Teachers must respond. In my work as a teacher of future kindergarten teachers and in my relations with kindergarten teachers in the field, my approach in the past has been to encourage them to balance the state, district, and school requirements with what they know is best for young children. Typically that meant doing their best to plan and deliver a "developmentally appropriate" program while making some accommodations for the academic expectations contained in state and district curriculum guides. I would try to give them tools for integrating instruction (e.g., thematic units, learning centers, and projects) and strategies for accomplishing the state/district objectives within those integrating approaches. Again, this was an attempt to balance essentially constructivist and behaviorist ways of thinking about kindergarten teaching. I now see this balance between two competing philosophies as too simplistic to take into account the complexity of what we now know about children, teaching, and the pressures of the standards movement.

Complicating teachers' concerns about accountability shovedown are shifts in the demographics that characterize our society and expectations that children

APPLICATIONS

Teachers will need to adjust their programs to be sure the needs of children with disabilities are met.

Imagine your principal has informed you that a child with muscular dystrophy has moved into the district and that he will be placed in your kindergarten classroom. In preparation for the new student's arrival, the principal has arranged a meeting that will be attended by you, the boy's parents, his preschool special education teacher, a physical therapist, and the district special education supervisor. To get ready for the meeting, list all the questions you will ask of each of the meeting participants. Be sure to ask about accommodations to ensure the child's inclusion in all aspects of classroom life.

with disabilities will be included in regular education classrooms. Demographic predictions for the first decade of the new millennium signal that children under six will continue to make up a major portion of those living in poverty, that so-called minority populations will in many areas become the majority or increase their majority status, and that the number of children for whom English is a second language will continue to increase (Washington & Andrews, 1998). This means that kindergarten teachers in virtually all public schools will be working with children from poor families, children from minority backgrounds, and/or children who don't speak English at home. It also means that kindergarten teachers in some schools will be teaching children living in these contexts almost exclusively.

In addition, current special education law requires that children identified for special services because of a disability receive those services in a regular education setting wherever possible. This means that teachers will need to adjust their programs to be sure the needs of children with disabilities are met.

I see these realities as opportunities, but I don't see them as easy to deal with, especially in the climate of standards-based reform. Working with children and families from diverse backgrounds is not a problem per se, but it certainly complicates the job of teaching kindergarten. Meeting the needs of diverse learners requires an even more complex balancing act on the part of teachers. The new kindergarten described here provides a framework for kindergarten that ensures *all* children can be successful at this critical stage in their school careers.

The new balance described in this book includes taking a head-on approach to making sure all kindergarten students are prepared to meet the

Teachers must find ways to ensure that all children are successful in kindergarten.

expectations of the accountability movement. That does not mean capitulating to behaviorist teaching strategies that ignore important areas of children's development, and it does not mean throwing away the powerful contributions of constructivist approaches. It does mean rethinking the place of elements like direct instruction and thematic units in kindergarten classrooms. It means taking seriously what kindergarten teachers tell me and what I see with my own eyes: new ways of teaching kindergarten are needed.

Closing Thoughts

I have tried to make the case that new approaches to teaching kindergarten are needed in order to address changes in the experience of childhood, enriched understandings of learning and development, and the challenges of the accountability movement. I believe teaching is a complex intellectual activity that requires the ability to bring together knowledge and understanding from a variety of sources to make good decisions that directly benefit children. I was trained to think of early childhood programs in either/or terms. Either a program was developmental or academic; either it was appropriate or inappropriate; either it was integrated or skills-based; either it was child-centered or subject-centered. It's time to redefine kindergarten teaching by challenging the dichotomous, either/or constructs that have characterized our thinking in the past. It's time to raise the status of teacher decision making to a more complex level than choosing between opposing alternatives or finding the balance point between two extremes. It's time to teach the child while meeting the standards—to stay focused on the needs, interests, and abilities of children while making sure that real substance is included in the curriculum and real learning is accomplished by each child.

In Western societies, we are socialized to believe that there is one right answer to every question, one correct solution to every problem, and one best approach to any situation. So it's understandable that we want clear and direct guidance on the best way to teach. Most of us come to early childhood teaching because we love children and enjoy the intrinsic rewards of working with them (Phillips & Hatch, 2000). Put the need for the best way to teach and the attraction of working with children together and you create a compelling case for the popularity of the "child-centered" approach. If we love children, what could be wrong with placing them at the center of everything we do? The answer may not be as simple as we would like. As I have argued above, there are no single best answers to the complex issues surrounding teaching, so expecting any approach to provide the optimum learning environment for all children may be expecting too much.

I am proposing that kindergarten teachers use all of the tools at their disposal to create learning opportunities that improve the life chances of all the children they teach. One of the strengths of early childhood education is the dedicated commitment of its teachers. Individuals selecting this profession are good at what they do in direct proportion to the joys they experience working with young children. To shift to a teaching approach that devalues early childhood teachers' love for children would be bad for teachers and children.

But a child-centered approach as it has been traditionally defined is no longer sufficient. Thinking of kindergarten in broader terms will allow us to focus the energy we get from our commitment to children and use our professional knowledge about children, development, teaching, and learning to help children succeed in the current school climate. What I describe in the chapters that follow are ways to keep the needs, abilities, and interests of children central to our considerations, while using new understandings of curriculum, teaching, and classroom organization to improve children's achievement—usually translated as standards.

The chapters that follow are organized around the questions that drive any good teacher's professional life: What do I teach? How do I teach? How do I organize and manage my classroom? and How will it all come together? I have tried to provide straightforward, detailed answers to each of these questions without ignoring the complexity of the ideas introduced above. My objective is to provide a solid framework on which individual kindergarten teachers can build successful programs in a variety of settings.

Chapter 2 is divided into sections based on the elements of curriculum that should be included in a kindergarten program: language arts, math, science, social studies, physical education, and the creative arts. Sections for each element include descriptions of the concepts, skills, operations, processes, understandings, and dispositions that make up the substance that should be taught. These descriptions are based on the latest recommendations from scholarly organizations, state and district curriculum guides, widely adopted texts, national reports that have examined best practices in the content areas, and published advice from experts in early childhood and each discipline. I want to provide new and experienced teachers with specific information about what ought to be in their kindergarten curriculum.

Content is presented as *a* curriculum rather than *the* curriculum. The idea is not to dictate what ought to be taught in every classroom, but to provide a complete description of what *could* be taught so that teachers have it as a ready reference for organizing what they teach and a source for comparison when they are confronted with implementing curricula prescribed by others. The presentation of each section is parallel. I provide a brief rationale for the importance of teaching each subject area, then describe the curriculum for that area. I remind the readers throughout that just because content needs to be specified within disciplinary boundaries does not mean that the content must be taught in a fragmented way or in isolation from content from other subject-matter areas.

Chapter 3 emphasizes the teacher's role as an active information processor and decision maker. I spell out options for teachers to consider as they design instructional approaches. A framework for decision making that provides a tool for examining and applying what is known in given situations is presented. Teaching strategies that follow from decisions about what kindergartners in different situations need are described. These strategies are presented on a continuum (from incidental to direct teaching) in an effort to help teachers see connections between possible teaching options and desirable outcomes. The goal is to bring balance to kindergarten teaching and move away from the idea that one teaching strategy fits all, that one teaching strategy is appropriate, or that one teaching strategy is most effective in accomplishing outcomes prescribed by others. The teacher is in the best position to know the optimum instructional approaches for particular children in particular contexts, and this chapter gives kindergarten teachers ways to make good decisions so that they can be sure each child's needs are being met at the same time they are doing all they can to ensure academic success. I conclude the chapter with concrete examples of how to deliver the content of the curriculum using the teaching strategies presented in the continuum.

In Chapter 4, the instructional balance introduced in Chapter 3 is complimented with an emphasis on balancing classroom organization and management. I use the concept of balance to help kindergarten teachers see their classroom organizer and manager roles as dynamic and complex rather than fixed and linear.

Human beings, including kindergarten children and their parents, respond when they see a sense of purpose behind what they are asked to do; and conversely, they resist when they cannot understand the purpose. The purpose of the new kindergarten ought to be to "learn a little every day." Decisions about how to use space and time and what activities to provide for whom should be based on the notion that the purpose is to learn. When teachers and students have a shared purpose, classroom discipline no longer means that teachers control children. In these classrooms, everyone is responsible for classroom order so that learning can happen. How to set up and foster kindergarten classrooms with such a purpose is the substance of this chapter. Special discussions on including children with disabilities and working with children who have difficulty taking responsibility are included. In addition, I outline several strategies for the ongoing collection of assessment data that meet the purposes of the classroom and discuss ways parents can be engaged as resources, allies, and partners in accomplishing school purposes. The chapter concludes with a discussion of how to deal with potential threats to classroom balance.

The final chapter looks at a week in a new kindergarten classroom. The object is to pull the ideas in the previous chapters together by providing a comprehensive example of one week's instruction in kindergarten. Descriptions of lessons, activities, centers, and assessments are presented to give teachers a concrete example of how they can integrate the ideas in the book into a meaningful whole around a theme—in this case, a study of winter. Curriculum areas described in Chapter 2, teaching strategies outlined in Chapter 3, and organization and management suggestions presented in Chapter 4 will be addressed. Recommendations for alternative ways to accomplish the aims of the new kindergarten conclude the chapter and book.

FOR YOUR CONSIDERATION

1. What are positive and negative potential outcomes for children who have experienced out-of-home care for several years prior to entering kindergarten?

2. What conflicts might exist for children socialized in postmodern families as they enter school settings characterized by mostly modern norms?

3. What elements (if any) of maturationist, behaviorist, and constructivist theories continue to have a place in contemporary kindergartens?

4. What is the place (if any) of systematic phonics instruction in kindergarten?

5. What should kindergarten teachers do in response to the pressures of accountability shovedown?

LEARNING ACTIVITIES

INDIVIDUAL ACTIVITIES

• Make a systematic analysis of how your childhood experiences are the same as and different from those of children today. In your analysis, include such domains as out-of-home care, family structure, media exposure, social values, stress, and school experiences.

• Interview a kindergarten teacher, asking him/her to describe school and district accountability expectations. Also, find out how the teacher responds to those expectations in the classroom.

SMALL GROUP ACTIVITIES

• Generate a list of core beliefs that your group thinks ought to guide kindergarten practices in any school, anywhere. Once your list is complete, examine each belief to be sure it fits kindergartens in urban and rural areas, rich and poor schools, majority and minority populations, children with and without disabilities, and native English speakers and English language learners.

• Analyze what's the same and what's different in Piaget's and Vygotsky's descriptions of how young children learn and develop. Make a list of ways kindergarten would be different if teachers applied Vygotsky's ideas about development and assessment.

Continues

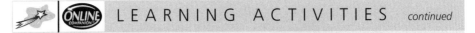

LEARNING ACTIVITIES   *continued*

LARGE GROUP ACTIVITIES

- Divide the class into four teams and assign one team each to identify learning principles associated with Vygotsky, Reggio Emilia, Project Spectrum, and *How People Learn*. After providing out-of-class time to gather information, have teams report five key principles from their assigned perspective. Record these principles on charts and look for similarities and differences across perspectives.

- Assign students to bring in examples of media targeted at children. Provide time for students to share their examples, then lead a discussion of the direct and indirect messages sent to children through the media. Explore the possible motives of those who produce the media, and discuss consequences of media consumption for children, schools, and society.

CHAPTER 2

What Do I Teach in the New Kindergarten?

KEY TERMS AND CONCEPTS

Curriculum

Objectives

Standards

Language Arts

- Reading

- Writing

- Speaking

- Listening

Mathematics

- Number and operations

- Algebra

- Geometry

- Measurement

- Data analysis

Science

- Life science

- Physical science

- Earth and space science

- Science processes

  - Observation

  - Classification

  - Hypothesizing

  - Investigation

  - Interpretation

  - Communication

Social Studies

- Self

- Family

- Community

Health

Physical Education

Art

Music

The old answer to "What do I teach in kindergarten?" was "socialization skills to get them ready for first grade." Kindergarten used to be thought

In the past, kindergarten was conceived as a buffer between home and "real" school.

of as a year of transition designed to help kids make the adjustment from being at home to being in school. The formal rigors of school were thought to begin in first grade, and kindergarten was usually conceived of as a kind of buffer between home and "real" school. Kindergarten teachers gradually introduced young children to the behavioral and learning expectations of school, but did so in a manner that emphasized development over learning. Curriculum elements like "pre-reading" or "pre-math" focused on developing "readiness to learn" as opposed to actual learning, and often even these elements were not organized into a formal curriculum.

For the reasons discussed on Chapter 1, all this has changed. Kindergarten maintains its place as the child's first experience with formal schooling, but it rarely represents the child's first out-of-home educational experience.

Kindergarten's function as the place where readiness is developed has been taken over by preschool programs and individual parents anxious for their children to have a head start on learning. While socialization into the world of the school will be an inherent function of kindergartens until we have universal public preschools, the expectation that children will learn real reading and math has moved down from first grade to kindergarten (Joyce, Hrycauk, & Calhoun, 2003).

In addition, other subject matter areas that make up the curricula of first grade and beyond are now formalized in the new kindergarten. Content from subjects like science, social studies, physical education, and the arts have often been included in kindergarten programs as a kind of backdrop for the interesting activities that teachers liked to do with their students. Teachers planned thematic units and set up learning centers through which children could explore science and social studies concepts, but the emphasis was on exploration and discovery, not on learning real science or social studies content. Similarly, physical education and the creative arts have been important parts of kindergartners' experiences in the past, but these areas were treated even more as curricular backdrop than as foreground. In the new kindergarten, language arts, math, science, social studies, physical education, and the creative arts *are* the curriculum. In broad strokes, these subject matter domains are what is taught. That doesn't mean that exploration is not important or that units, projects, and learning centers are not appropriate. It does mean that real reading, real math, and real content from the other subject matter areas will move to center stage in the kindergarten curriculum.

In this chapter, I lay out a detailed curriculum for kindergarten. This is not meant to be *the* curriculum for kindergarten; it is intended to be a comprehensive example of what could be included. This curriculum represents a significant shift in my own thinking on how to help others learn to teach kindergarten. My approach in the past has been to teach prospective teachers how to plan interesting thematic units, develop engaging projects, and prepare effective learning centers. I always made my students find kindergarten guidelines in district and/or state curriculum documents and encouraged them to look at curriculum guidelines from professional organizations and widely published textbook series, but these sources were always secondary to their own ideas about how to make learning processes interesting and engaging. This shift represents a change in the balance between process and content. It means moving from creating terrific learning activities that should include some substance to teaching important content through a variety of terrific activities. Both process and content remain important; but substance takes a much more prominent place in the planning I now encourage.

APPLICATIONS

This shift means moving from creating terrific learning activities that should include some substance to teaching important content through a variety of terrific activities.

Imagine you have been asked to present a talk to a local grandparents club that is interested in volunteering in schools. They want to know what kinds of things kindergartners are learning. As part of your presentation, you want to give them a sense of the substance on the kindergarten curriculum as well as a taste of the activities used to teach that substance. Write the outline for your talk and include descriptions of several activities that demonstrate the place of content in your program.

Given this shift to placing content in the foreground, it makes sense to me to organize a complete sample curriculum based on the kinds of sources I have traditionally directed my students to find. The concepts, skills, operations, and understandings that make up the curriculum sections that follow are based on my synthesis of information from state and district curriculum guides, guidelines from professional organizations, scopes and sequences from widely adopted textbook series, national reports on best practices in the content areas, and published materials from independent early childhood and subject matter experts. Of course, new teachers must meet the curricular expectations of the schools, districts, and states in which they teach. While there should be considerable overlap between what I present below and what is expected in the schools, teachers must know and teach the kindergarten content they were hired to cover. Teachers who understand and buy into the premises of this book should have no trouble adjusting to the curriculum expectations of particular schools or school systems.

I am intentionally separating the issues of "what to teach" and "how to teach." Both are critical to effective kindergarten programs, but for me, the new kindergarten means a shift from focusing on creating engaging activities to a greater emphasis on **curriculum**—the "what to teach" part. Chapter 3 is all about ways to teach, and those ways include many of the approaches kindergarten teachers have developed for keeping children interested and motivated. This chapter lays out the curriculum elements that need to be taught; figuring out the best ways to teach them is left for later.

I have purposely resisted describing curriculum elements in terms of **objectives** or **standards.** I want to provide an organized list of elements that should be taught in kindergarten (i.e., a curriculum). This is information new teachers need in order to conceptualize and plan effective kindergarten programs. I don't want to identify particular behaviors that will signal when children have learned particular content; and I don't want to specify the level at which each objective should be mastered. Objectives and standards are a fact of life in the new kindergarten, and teachers would be foolish to ignore them, but when objectives and standards become the curriculum, learning becomes disconnected and fragmented, and the purpose for being in school shifts from learning important skills and concepts to performing well on narrowly defined tasks. Implementing the curriculum described here offers a way to help students accomplish the objectives and meet the standards without caving in to a system that distorts what children need to know, devalues learning as an important human activity, and places unnecessary pressure on teachers and children (Hatch, 2002). As instruction and assessment are discussed in later chapters, these issues will be taken up in detail. For now, the curriculum will be described as the content that should be taught in kindergarten.

The rest of this chapter is divided into sections devoted to each major subject matter area in the kindergarten curriculum. The presentation of each section is parallel. I provide an overview of each curriculum area and a brief rationale for why it's important to include it in kindergarten. A curriculum outline is pre-

APPLICATIONS

When objectives and standards *become* the curriculum, learning becomes disconnected and fragmented.

Imagine that you and the other kindergarten teachers at your school have been told that the district elementary curriculum supervisor will be checking lesson plans, observing in classrooms, and meeting with individual kindergarten teachers over the next two weeks. You and your coworkers decide to get together to plan how to get ready for the supervisor's visit. Your task before the meeting with your colleagues is to provide an explanation for how the state standards for kindergarten are being addressed in your program. Outline the basic elements of your explanation, including a rationale for why you teach the way you do; then describe some activities that you and your colleagues use to ensure that the standards are being addressed.

sented in each area, then descriptions of curriculum elements to be taught are spelled out in terms that new teachers can understand. (Note: elements from the curriculum outline are italicized in places they are explained in the text.)

Language Arts

Reading, writing, speaking, and listening—the language arts—are interconnected. All are centered on the basic characteristic that distinguishes humans from other animals: the ability to communicate. In order to participate fully in life, people need to be proficient communicators. They need to be able to share meaning with others through oral and written communication. Nothing is more important in schooling at any level than helping students become better communicators. They must acquire the ability to be effective speakers, efficient listeners, able readers, and competent writers. If they can't participate in the verbal and text-based communication around them, they will be relegated to the sidelines of life.

Not every kindergarten student will learn to read, but all children will move forward in the development of their language arts capabilities. A big part of the folklore of primary school is that children learn to read in first grade, and some would push that expectation down into kindergarten. This would be a mistake, one that could damage the life chances of untold numbers of young children. It is part of the either-or logic that has dominated past thinking: that is, either *all* kids should be taught to read in kindergarten or *all* children should wait until first grade to begin formal reading instruction. Teachers, school systems, parents, and policy makers who set up the expectation that young children fail if they do not learn to read in kindergarten guarantee that vast numbers of children will start their school careers labeled as failures. I treat reading as a key curriculum area imbedded within the related content of the language arts. I expect to provide kindergarten children with activities that will teach them a great deal about reading, writing, speaking, and listening. I expect that what they learn in kindergarten will move them closer to becoming effective communicators, capable of full participation in the demands of social and economic life in the twenty-first century. Some kindergartners will learn to read, all will move forward in their reading development.

In the following sections, the language arts curriculum is described following the outline in Figure 2–1. Sections on reading, writing, speaking, and listening content include the elements that make up an appropriate language arts curriculum for kindergarten. Elements are described in straightforward terms that should be familiar to kindergarten teachers, but these descriptions are not

READING

| phonemic awareness
| alphabetic principle
| print conventions
| correspondence between spoken
  and written words
| environmental print
| letters of the alphabet
| letter sound correspondence
| rhymes
| sight words
| decoding
| word families
| vocabulary
| comprehension
| simple text readings

WRITING

| first and last name
| upper and lower case letters
| writing conventions
| sight words
| dictated messages and stories
| invented spelling
| conventional spelling

SPEAKING

| vocabulary
| story retelling
| grammatical constructions
| sentence patterns
| descriptive language

LISTENING

| vocabulary
| comprehension
| directions
| attending to oral readings

Figure 2–1 | Language Arts Curriculum Outline

meant to be comprehensive treatments of complex concepts, understandings, and skills. More information on each is readily available from school district materials, state- and district-adopted textbook series, books, journal articles, and other professional sources, including reputable Internet sites.

Reading

When children learn *phonemic awareness*, they come to understand that spoken words are made up of sounds that can be separated and manipulated. This is a basic concept on which learning to read depends. Having phonemic awareness is not the same as knowing phonics (i.e., letter sound relationships and decoding—addressed later), but learning phonics principles and other elements of reading will be meaningless unless children first acquire the awareness that words they can say and understand are constructed from a consistent set of identifiable sounds.

Understanding the *alphabetic principle* is not the same as reciting or knowing the alphabet. Building on phonemic awareness, the alphabetic principle is another core understanding that forms the basis for further reading development. When children understand the alphabetic principle, they know that the sequence of letters in written words stands for the sequence of sounds in spoken words. In order to apply the alphabetic principle, children do not have to know all the letters and letter-sound relationships; they need only understand that those relationships exist. Unless that understanding is in place, further reading development will be difficult.

Print conventions are basic concepts related to how text works. They include understanding what letters, words, and sentences are and that meaning in books comes from reading the words in the text. Concepts such as reading pages from top to bottom and from left to right, and reading books from front to back are print conventions. Learning the parts of a book and the roles of authors and illustrators is important to developing basic concepts about how text works. The basics of capitalization and punctuation are additional print conventions that are appropriately introduced in kindergarten.

An important step in reading development comes when children see the *correspondence between spoken and written words*. This is the basic knowledge that what they say can be written down, and conversely, that what they see when they look at text is what someone else could be saying out loud. Reading and writing should be taught as communication—sharing meaning between readers and writers in the same way that speakers and listeners communicate in face-to-face conversation. That text is speech written down is a powerful lesson.

Environmental print is text that is found all around us. Virtually all children come to kindergarten with the ability to read the packages that hold their favorite foods, the logos on their favorite toys, and the signs for their favorite restaurants. Capitalizing on and extending this knowledge in the classroom is a powerful tool for expanding literacy understandings in kindergarten.

Learning to recognize and name the *letters of the alphabet* is an important part of the kindergarten reading curriculum. In order to learn to operate effectively on print, children need to be able to say the alphabet (distinguishing each letter from the next, not just singing the alphabet song), to pick out individual letters when named, to identify letters when presented, and to match upper- and lowercase letters. As we will see below, identifying, naming, and matching should be coupled with learning to write the upper- and lowercase letters.

For kindergartners who have acquired phonemic awareness, understand the alphabetic principle, and are learning the letters of the alphabet, it makes sense to introduce *letter-sound correspondence*. Here we are teaching children the sounds that particular consonants and vowels usually make. In kindergarten, this most often takes the form of helping children associate letters with sounds through the use of familiar words that begin with the target letter (e.g., b says the /b/ sound like you hear at the start of "ball"). Some kindergarten children will have difficulty learning letter-sound combinations, but many will learn to produce the sound when given a regular consonant or short vowel, identify the letter when given the sound, and name other words that begin with the same sound.

Identifying and making *rhymes* is a skill that is important to teaching children how sounds work within words and how recognizing patterns can make reading easier. Rhyming in kindergarten should be taught as words that sound alike at the end, and children should have experiences that help them to distinguish words that rhyme from those that don't and to think of their own words that rhyme with given words.

Sight words, or high-frequency words, are those that appear most often in our language and need to be read by sight as opposed to sounded out. Several lists of such words are published, and most school systems and textbook series have their own lists. It is appropriate to introduce sight words in kindergarten and give children activities that allow them to practice reading these words automatically.

Kindergartners who are comfortable with letter-sound correspondence are ready to practice the basic processes of *decoding*, or sounding out, words. Blending the sounds in one-syllable words that follow the phonics rules is a good place to start (e.g., consonant-vowel-consonant patterns in words like "pan" and "fat"). The object is to teach children that they can use their knowledge of letter-sound relationships to figure out what unfamiliar words are by blending sounds together in a systematic way.

Teaching children about *word families* can also enhance reading improvement. Word families are sets of words that are related because they are identical except for one letter (usually the initial consonant for kindergartners). The idea is to teach children that if they can read one word (e.g., "pot"), they can easily read several words in the pot family (e.g., cot, dot, got, hot, jot, lot, not, rot, tot) just by substituting the sound of a new initial consonant. Word families are powerful tools because they help unlock reading by linking with rhymes, sound-letter correspondence, and decoding to show children how text can be structured in patterned ways.

Vocabulary is central to literacy development and is addressed in all of the language arts areas. Understanding that words carry meaning and learning the importance of comprehending the meaning of written words are basic goals of

 APPLICATIONS

Comprehension instruction focuses on listening comprehension in which children participate in shared book experiences, then reflect on their understandings.

Imagine that you want to engage parents in a project to accelerate their kindergartners' reading development. Your aim is to encourage parents to read to children on a daily basis and to teach parents to talk to their children about the books they are reading in a effort to improve listening comprehension skills. Make a handout that you could use at a parent information meeting introducing your project and asking for parents' support. In the handout, provide a brief rationale for reading with children and include a list of sample questions that parents could use as a model for talking with their children about the books they have shared.

vocabulary instruction in kindergarten reading. At this stage, children's speaking and listening vocabularies will far outpace their reading vocabularies, so building connections between words they use in their spoken language and words they are learning to read and write is important.

Like vocabulary, *comprehension* in reading is closely tied to comprehension in the other language arts. Since children are limited in the text they are able to read on their own, most comprehension instruction focuses on listening comprehension in which children participate in shared book experiences, then reflect on their understanding of what is happening in the stories they are "reading." Some of those understandings are detailed below under comprehension in listening—they include elements such as sequence, story recall, and prediction.

Teachers need to give children a chance to use their developing literacy abilities with *simple text readings*. Kindergartners should be using their emerging literacy skills to read real text. They can read back text that they have dictated to teachers or others, they can read predictable books that have been shared frequently with the class, and they can read controlled vocabulary readers that match up with their reading development. Few things in teaching compare with the pure joy of being with children when they discover that they can read. Children don't know they can read unless they are operating on real text, as opposed to practicing the parts of reading in isolation. All of the elements above may be important to reading development, but if children don't actually

Writing is the expressive side of text-based communication.

bring them all together in the act of getting meaning from text, those elements have dubious value.

Writing

Writing should be thought of as the expressive side of text-based communication, and children learn to express themselves in writing at the same time they are learning the receptive side of written communication through reading. Children learn to write *as* (not after) they learn to read. Among the first words they learn to read and write are their *first and last names*. These should be taught using the standard manuscript handwriting model adopted by the school district and using uppercase letters for the first letter in each name and lowercase letters for the rest.

At the same time they are introduced in reading activities, children should be given opportunities to practice writing *upper- and lowercase letters*. Some children will come to kindergarten with advanced handwriting skills, and some will not be writing legibly by the end of the year. Those differences can be explained in terms of experience and psychomotor development, and young children should not be stigmatized because they have difficulty with the complex tasks of handwriting. Still, all children should be learning to identify and write the letters of the alphabet at whatever level they are able.

Just as they need to become familiar with print conventions to be able to read, so do children need to learn *writing conventions* to be able to communicate effectively in writing. Learning that writing moves from left to right and usually begins at the top of the page and moves down is important, as are gaining an awareness of the purposes of basic capitalization and punctuation rules. Writing is meant to be read, and writing conventions should be taught as tools for helping children make their writing readable to others.

Kindergartners should be writing the words they can read, so *sight words* will be among the early words that children can read and write. The same logic applies to writing the words used to teach decoding skills and the word family concept. Writing instruction will make sense to young children if it is taught as expressive communication, the mirror of reading. Children should be writing the same words they are learning to read.

At the same time children are learning writing conventions, they should be creating their own expressive communication through *dictated messages and stories.* Writing development happens in identifiable stages that begin with drawing and scribbling and move to producing conventional text (Schickedanz, 1999). Having children draw pictures, then writing about what they have drawn is a powerful way to support writing development. It teaches children that text is spoken language written down, that meaning is carried in text, and that they can produce meaningful communication that can be understood by others who are not present. Children can dictate individually and in groups, and they should, over time, be encouraged to write as much as possible on their own, leaving teachers or other able writers to record the dictated intentions they could not write without assistance.

Invented spelling happens when children use their developing knowledge of letter-sound correspondence to write words the way they sound to them. It represents a significant positive step in writing development. Children often write initial consonant sounds with which they are familiar, using those to stand for whole words. Later they usually add final consonants, then begin experimenting with vowels. Invented spelling should be thought of as a transition between scribbling and conventional spelling. It should not be the teacher's goal to get every child to do invented spelling, but to move every child toward conventional writing with the expectation that many children will use invented spelling as a valuable tool along the way.

Instruction in *conventional spelling* can have positive effects on learning to read and write. Kindergartners are not up to weekly spelling tests like those many of us took in elementary school, but spelling can be taught in rudimentary ways in kindergarten. Children can learn that words are spelled the same way every time we see them and that they will learn to spell them the same way every time so that others will be able to read their writing. It makes sense that the same words children are reading and writing will be the ones they will be learning to spell correctly.

Speaking

Speaking is the expressive side of oral communication, and kindergartners should learn that being understood is a vital part of participating in the social events that make up most of their lives. Spoken *vocabulary* development is tied to learning vocabulary through reading and writing. Improving the speaking vocabularies of young children opens the door to accelerated learning in the other language arts and across the curriculum. Cognitive theorists such as Vygotsky (1962) argue that learning to think is directly linked to the development of language, so an emphasis on vocabulary development in early schooling may be critical to general cognitive development as well as learning how to effectively use spoken and written language.

Story retelling is the skill of being able to relate a familiar piece of text in your own words. In kindergarten, this usually means children "read" books that have been read to the class several times. They use their own words to tell the story while looking at the pictures as the pages of the book are turned. Students also retell stories when they convey the meaning of a text they know without having the book as a prompt and when they participate with others in role playing story events. The processes involved in story retelling help children learn a great deal about speaking, vocabulary, recall, sequence, character, plot, and other elements of comprehension and story grammar.

Kindergarten children experience rapid language development. Their spoken language sometimes reveals places where their understandings of *grammatical constructions* are outpaced by their desire and need to communicate freely. As new elements of conventional grammar are introduced, it is common for children at this age to overgeneralize these elements, applying them even when they don't fit. For example, when children learn that "ed" endings signal past tense, they often apply "ed" to irregular verbs ("runned" for "ran" or "goed" for "went"). Kindergarten teachers should see these overgeneralizations as evidence of what children are learning and build on that learning to help them begin to master the complexities of English grammar.

Helping children make sense when they speak because they need to be understood is the reason for spoken language instruction. Speaking in sentences and recognizing and using *sentence patterns* are important elements of being understood. In kindergarten, sentence patterns for statements, questions, and exclamations are sufficient. Children can learn the general characteristics of sentence patterns and begin to apply those characteristics in their own speech.

Learning to use *descriptive language* is another goal of a kindergarten spoken language curriculum. Here we want young speakers to be able to help others have a clearer understanding of their communication efforts. The most obvious place to emphasize is helping students use adjectives to give listeners a more specific account of what speakers are describing, but descriptive language for young children also involves helping them include more details and more elaborate explanations so that listeners have a clearer idea of what they are trying to say.

Listening

Listening is the fourth language art, and it should receive active attention in the curriculum. Among the language arts, listening is usually the one that receives the least direct attention throughout schooling, including kindergarten. As with the other language arts, listening should be taught as communication—receptive verbal communication. Understanding the verbal messages that others are sending is vital to full participation in school and in the world at large. Having an adequate listening *vocabulary* is essential to successful verbal interchange. If people cannot understand the words others are saying, they cannot be full participants in the social interactions that define a large part of their lives. Kindergarten is an appropriate place to systematically build vocabulary in all the language arts.

As with reading, *comprehension* is essential to effective listening. Since young children are just learning to read, much of the instruction related to the development of comprehension skills is tied to helping them respond to stories and other text that is read to them. As they listen to what is read by others, they use the same cognitive processes they will use when they are able to read the texts independently. Comprehension skills introduced in kindergarten include sequence (what happened first, second, last), prediction (what will happen next), cause and effect (what made that happen), comparison (what's the same, different), and recall details (who, what, when, where).

Learning to understand and follow simple *directions* is an important element in the listening curriculum. In the past, some teachers have reduced "following directions" to evaluating how well children do what teachers tell them to do. Here, we are talking about listening, memory, and information processing skills—not attitude or compliance. Kindergartners need practice learning to listen to directions with two and (later) three steps, then immediately carrying out the directions in succession. Listening, sequencing, and short-term memory skills are involved in carrying out a set of tasks like these; and real instruction and practice are required to get many kindergartners to this point.

Shared reading is described in Chapter 3 as a complex teaching strategy that involves children in the act of reading with more able readers, usually their teachers. In large measure, effective shared reading depends on children's abilities to attend to oral readings of stories and other texts. Reading to and with children is an essential part of every kindergarten day, and, if children are unable to listen attentively to the stories, poems, and other texts that are read to them, their opportunities for learning to read and write will be significantly limited. Learning how books work, how text is organized, how to get meaning from words and pictures, and how wonderful books are ought to be major aims of the kindergarten language arts curriculum. Being able to participate in shared reading, including being able to listen to and understand what others are reading, is essential to accomplishing those objectives.

Mathematics

> *For people to participate fully in society, they must know basic mathematics. Citizens who cannot reason mathematically are cut off from whole realms of human endeavor. Innumeracy deprives them not only of opportunity but also of competence in everyday tasks. . . . All young Americans must learn to think mathematically, and they must think mathematically to learn.*

This is the powerful conclusion of the Mathematics Learning Study Committee of the National Research Council (Kilpatrick, Swafford, & Findell, 2001, p. 1). In the new kindergarten, children have a chance to establish a firm foundation in the kind of math they'll need to participate in society. At this writing, the focus from national to local levels is on promoting literacy in early childhood classrooms. While no one questions the importance of teaching children to read and write, a balanced program that includes mathematics and the other subject-matter areas is what is needed in the long run (Jacobson, 2001).

In traditional kindergartens, math was "caught, not taught." The idea was to include math concepts and operations (like counting and simple addition) as part of daily classroom activities, but not to teach math in direct or systematic ways. Many children, especially those who came to school already understanding numbers and how they work, did fine in programs based on this incidental approach. Others, however, did not "catch" the math knowledge necessary to provide a foundation for later math learning and found themselves behind from the beginning. Other, more skill-based programs have attempted to cover so many mathematics concepts in such fragmented and disconnected ways that children learn very little and can apply even less.

A joint position statement on early childhood mathematics issued by the National Association for the Education of Young Children and the National Council for the Teachers of Mathematics (NAEYC/NCTM, 2002) parallels the approach I am advocating here. The statement calls for "intentionally organized learning experiences" that ensure children "encounter concepts in depth and in a logical sequence" (p. 4). Chapter 3 focuses on ways to intentionally organize math learning experiences, and the sections that follow are my synthesis of what should be included in a math curriculum that has depth and a logical sequence.

Figure 2–2 is an outline of the mathematics curriculum elements. Elements are organized into five categories identified by the National Council for Teachers

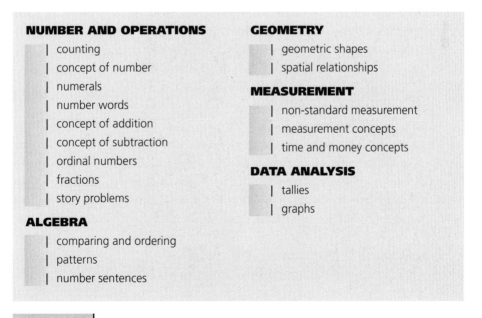

NUMBER AND OPERATIONS
| counting
| concept of number
| numerals
| number words
| concept of addition
| concept of subtraction
| ordinal numbers
| fractions
| story problems

ALGEBRA
| comparing and ordering
| patterns
| number sentences

GEOMETRY
| geometric shapes
| spatial relationships

MEASUREMENT
| non-standard measurement
| measurement concepts
| time and money concepts

DATA ANALYSIS
| tallies
| graphs

Figure 2–2 | Mathematics Curriculum Outline

of Mathematics: number and operations; algebra; geometry; measurement; and data analysis (NCTM, 2000). While some kindergarten teachers may be uneasy thinking about teaching algebra or data analysis to young children, as will become evident, the kindergarten math concepts in each of the five NCTM categories are right on target for five- and six-year-olds and provide a solid foundation for the further development of mathematics understanding.

Number and operations

Initial *counting* for young children is parallel to singing the alphabet song or reciting a simple prayer. At first, they learn to say the words as a rote memory exercise; later, they come to understand the meaning behind the words and are able to apply their counting skills to figure out how many objects are in a set. Learning to count is essential to the development of mathematics understanding. Without counting skills, children will not develop number concepts and have no way to understand or perform even simple math operations. Many children enter school with some counting skill, but most need instruction and practice to learn to count meaningfully. Many report cards reflect the expectation that students will be able to count to 20 by the end of kindergarten. Again, I don't want to set an arbitrary standard. Some children will be able to count to 100 and beyond, others will have trouble with the teen numbers and/or remembering the names for the decade numbers (20, 30, 40 . . .). Once children understand the logic and consistency of counting, many kindergarten teachers introduce counting by 10s, 5s, and sometimes 2s. Since counting is vital to further math learning, we should take kindergartners as far as they can go with their counting abilities, while remembering that not all children will be ready to accomplish the same things.

When children learn to count objects in sets and see that three books, three friends, three balls, or three anythings will always be three in number, they are developing the *concept of number*. Understanding that they can determine the quantities of objects in a set by counting is a big cognitive step. Young children learn to count sets of objects by moving them or touching them, but they do not automatically understand that the last number they say when counting out a set of objects is the number of objects in that set. This and other math concepts need to be explicitly taught and practiced.

Numerals are the numbers written down, the mathematical symbols that stand for the names of the numbers. Just as alphabet letters are the building blocks of written language, so are numerals the essential symbols of mathematical understanding. Just as they must know the letters of the alphabet, so do children need to be able to recognize and write numerals. It makes sense that as their counting skills advance and concepts of number develop, children should get used to seeing teachers record the products of counting by writing numerals on the board, on charts, on children's papers, and so on. Later, children will make their own records of their counting, comparing, adding, and subtracting efforts by writing the numerals themselves. This will not happen for most children unless they have been taught to recognize and write the numerals. As with the letters of the alphabet, learning to recognize and write the numerals requires instruction, practice, and feedback.

Number words are the numerals written as words. As numerals are learned and literacy skills are developed, number words can be included in sight word exercises, on word walls, and in children's other reading and writing activities. As children's math and literacy skills advance, it is appropriate to help them see the connections between quantities, numerals, and number words. The basic understanding you want them to have is that what they can count can be recorded as numerals and that these numerals can also be expressed as written words.

The *concept of addition* should be formally taught in kindergarten. As children become comfortable counting objects in sets, it is a natural next step to learn how to combine sets and determine how many objects they have all together. We are talking about learning what addition is and how it works, not about an endless stream of worksheets filled with simple addition problems or about flashcards that expect children to master addition facts. Addition is combining sets, and the sequence for teaching addition should follow from counting objects in sets, recording those numbers as numerals, comparing numbers of objects in sets, putting sets of objects together, counting them to find the total, then recording the results as number sentences. As these skills are introduced, proper mathematical terms such as "add," "plus," "sum," "total," and "equals" are used along with the more familiar language of putting sets together to find out "how many all together." Teaching what addition is will progress slowly, taking most of the year for many children, and some will not be able to grasp the addition concept completely during kindergarten.

The *concept of subtraction* is the inverse of addition, but is more difficult for children to understand. Subtracting is about separating sets—taking one set of objects away from a larger set and counting what's left. It is much easier to demonstrate two distinct sets being joined than to show children how part of one set is separated from another. Still, introducing subtraction in kindergarten is important, and some children will be ready to comprehend the mathematical logic of "take away." As with addition and other math concepts, the instructional sequence should lead from concrete experience guided by the teacher to written descriptions of actual subtraction activities, and the language of subtraction ("subtract," "minus," and "equals") should be introduced at the same time more common-sense descriptors are used.

Ordinal numbers are used to express order (as in "first," "second," and "third"). Kindergartners use ordinals in their everyday speech as they talk about who came in first or second in a race or about their siblings and friends in third or fourth grade. They also use ordinals in class to count the days of the month during calendar time. It is appropriate to formally teach ordinals, building on their prior knowledge and experience to help them count using ordinals and recognize some of the ordinal words as part of their sight word vocabulary development. It is also important to connect ordinal counting with sequence skills in language arts, helping students see ties between ordinals and what happened first, second, and last in stories.

Fractions in kindergarten will be limited to seeing parts of a whole (as opposed to seeing fractional parts of sets). Using regular geometric shapes such as circles, squares, and rectangles, teachers can show children that whole shapes can be divided into two, three, or four equal parts and that each part represents a fraction of the whole. In kindergarten, we are trying to help children begin to see whole-part relationships and get used to the language and notation of fractions (1/2, 1/3, 1/4). These basic conceptual and representational understandings are important to later, more complex, mathematics learning.

Mathematics is often taught as an abstract special language that requires special thinking. In the new kindergarten, we want all learning, mathematics learning included, to be as meaningful as possible. *Story problems* are used throughout most math instruction to help students apply the abstract math knowledge they are learning. Story problems usually take the form of imaginary written situations in which students must use information provided in the text to figure out what math operations to plug in. Story problems in kindergarten (and at all grade levels, if I were in charge) should not be about applying abstract math algorithms to imaginary situations, but should be about taking situations that are all around us and using the math we are learning to figure out answers to real questions. They should be as much a device for teaching concepts, operations, and algorithms as they are a mechanism for applying what's supposedly already learned. In kindergarten, this means that planned, organized teaching includes making stories of real situations that build in math skills and understandings. This approach makes math real and meaningful, giving children a sense of connection to their own developing mathematics understanding.

Algebra

Algebra in kindergarten? Yes, if it means teaching young children the patterns of thinking that lead to algebraic reasoning. *Comparing and ordering* represent two such patterns of thinking. Building on their developing capacities to sort and classify objects, children can learn to compare and order objects and sets based on particular characteristics. When two objects or two sets are examined, they can be compared; when three or more are studied, they can be ordered. Comparison of objects involves measurement-related relationships such as larger/smaller, longer/shorter, higher/lower, and heavier/lighter. The abilities to count and to understand number are required before set comparison is possible. To compare sets, children also need to understand the concepts of more than, less than, and equal to and be able to see how numbers are related. Ordering objects involves complex understandings that will allow children to order objects from largest to smallest, longest to shortest, and so on. Ordering sets is even more complex because it involves figuring out how many objects are in three or more sets, then ordering them from least to most or most to least. This is no easy task, and some kindergartners will have difficulty. Still, many will be ready to apply their developing math abilities through adult-supported comparison and ordering activities.

Being able to recognize and reproduce *patterns* is a general cognitive skill that is related to many subject matter areas, including mathematics. The cognitive processes involved (attending to different attributes, comparing, seeing relationships, and sequencing) are linked to the foundations of algebraic thinking. Kindergartners can learn to identify simple (two- and three-part patterns) in their surroundings and can practice reproducing and creating patterns in their work with blocks, beads, rhymes, and numbers.

Number sentences mentioned earlier, deserve special attention here because number sentences are a critical part of algebraic notation. One of the first concepts of algebra taught to older children is that both sides of an equation must be equal. Learning to express relationships in number sentences that follow that rule is essential to all higher mathematical understanding. As addition and subtraction concepts are introduced in kindergarten, helping children see that operations can be represented as number sentences (e.g., $3 + 1 = 4$; $4 - 1 = 3$) and that values on both sides of the equal sign must be equivalent is important math learning.

Geometry

Teaching two-dimensional *geometric shapes* has been a mainstay in kindergarten for a long time. Helping children learn to recognize, draw, and identify

Children extend their knowledge of measurement concepts in kindergarten.

the characteristics of circles, squares, triangles, and rectangles continues to have an important place in kindergarten math instruction. Children apply a great deal of understanding when they can articulate differences between geometric shapes in terms of lines, sides, and angles.

Spatial relationships are central to geometric thinking and to general understandings of how objects are related in space. Exploring relationships such as over, under, behind, in front of, left, and right involve children in thinking about the geometry of physical space, but they also extend conceptual and vocabulary knowledge. As has been mentioned several times, connections among elements across subject matter areas should be evident throughout the curriculum. Chapter 3 discusses how to teach in ways that maximize the benefits of those connections.

Measurement

Children's ability to measure and understand measurement concepts builds directly on their developing capacities to compare and order. Measurement provides tools for accurately determining relative length, width, height, weight, and volume. Initial measuring attempts in kindergarten usually involve the use of *nonstandard measurement*. Linear measurements are made using familiar objects such as hands, paper clips, and children's own bodies. Children are taught to determine how many paper clips long their crayon boxes are or how many hands tall the bookcase is. The idea is to teach the concept of measurement and the rudimentary procedures for accomplishing it. Teaching children to measure relative weight means giving them directed experiences comparing objects using simple balance scales. Different sized containers can be used to teach children how to compare volume.

Children extend their knowledge of *measurement concepts* in kindergarten. Even though most kindergartners will not be ready to use the tools of standard measurement, they should be introduced to those tools and see their relationship to what is being measured. For example, clocks, watches, and calendars measure time; thermometers measure temperature; tape measures, rulers, yardsticks, and metersticks measure length; scales measure weight; measuring cups measure volume. At the same time, kindergartners should also be learning associated measurement-related concepts (time, temperature, length, width, height, weight, and volume) and the words used to compare measured quantities (earlier/later, hotter/colder, longer/shorter, wider/thinner, higher/lower, heavier/lighter, more/less).

Children should be introduced to *money and time concepts* as part of the math curriculum in kindergarten. They can learn to identify and name the coins (penny through quarter) and start to match each coin with its value in cents. Children should work with calendars and clocks to begin to see how time is represented and measured. They can learn to recite the names of the months and days of the week, and see how ordinals represent the sequence of days each month. Most will learn how to tell time to the hour.

Data analysis

Data analysis for kindergartners is limited to learning how to record data in simple but accurate ways so that comparisons can be made. *Tallies* are a simple way to use symbolic representations to represent real objects or phenomena. When children make tally marks, they learn the importance of applying principles of one-to-one correspondence—making one and only one mark for each observed element to be recorded. Tallies can then be counted and totals represented as numbers, numerals, and number words. They can also be converted into other forms for representing data, especially graphs.

Graphs can take many forms in kindergarten, but they must be organized in ways that make analysis possible for young children. Simple graphs in which actual objects are laid out side by side so that direct observation and counting can be used to compare quantities are the place to start. Children should be involved in making the graphs they are expected to analyze, and lots of real objects, pictures of real objects, or symbols that represent real objects should be used to make graphs before abstract graphs are introduced. As children become aware that quantities (often recorded as tallies) can be represented on a graph using lines, bars, or areas, they can start to analyze data by making comparisons using the abstract representations on graphs. Data analysis usually takes the form of comparing two or three amounts. For example, more children said they like vanilla than chocolate ice cream, or we had more cloudy than sunny or rainy days in March.

Science

Science, like mathematics, is often "perceived and presented as too formal, too abstract, too theoretical—in short, too hard for young children and their teachers" (Johnson, 1999, p. 19). In most classrooms for older children, science has traditionally been taught as if the teacher were the authority and students were supposed to soak up scientific knowledge reading the textbook and taking lecture notes. In early childhood, constructivist approaches sometimes moved the teacher too far to the other extreme, leaving children with too much responsibility for constructing their own (sometimes idiosyncratic) scientific understandings. In the new kindergarten, science has an important place in the overall curriculum, and students are active participants in learning real science content and developing their capacities to use real scientific processes, with the direction of their teachers.

The American Association for the Advancement of Science (AAAS) has been engaged in an ongoing project designed to improve science teaching and learning. As part of this effort, called Project 2061, AAAS (2001) has taken the stance that covering fewer topics with greater clarity and depth is a better approach to science teaching than trying to cover too much content at a superficial level. The same emphasis on studying fewer science concepts at more depth guided the National Research Council (NRC, 1996) as they put together *National Science Education Standards.* I am against curricula that are "a mile wide and an inch deep" (Bransford, Brown, & Cocking, 1999, p. xvii). I like the notion that sometimes less can be more and have tried to apply it throughout this chapter, including the science curriculum.

The national science standards from NRC have had a powerful influence on science education since their publication. As I searched the science curric-

APPLICATIONS

Covering fewer topics with greater clarity and depth is a better approach to science teaching than trying to cover too much content at a superficial level.

Imagine that your state legislature has mandated that 75% of instructional time in all K–3 classrooms must be devoted to teaching reading and math. This means that the remaining 25% must be divided among all the other subject matter areas, including science. Given these constraints, identify the specific curriculum elements in science that you will address in your kindergarten curriculum over the course of a year. As you are considering the science curriculum, look for opportunities to integrate science content with substance from the other curricular areas, including reading and math.

ula of state departments of education, looked at the latest science textbooks, and studied the literature on early childhood science, the NRC standards seemed to be everywhere. Because they are so widely used (and because they make sense), I have organized my presentation of science content using the content descriptors that fit kindergarten science: life science, physical science, and earth and space science (NRC, 1996, p. 106). The elements under those content organizers and the processes that follow (outlined in Figure 2–3)

SCIENCE CONTENT

Life Science
| animals
| plants
| the body

Physical Science
| matter
| sound, heat, and light

Earth and Space Science
| weather
| land and water
| the sky

SCIENCE PROCESSES
| observation
| classification
| hypothesizing
| investigation
| interpretation
| communication

Figure 2-3 | Science Curriculum Outline

represent a synthesis of information from a variety of sources and my own experiences and understandings.

Science content

Life science

The study of *animals* is a basic content area of the kindergarten life science curriculum. Children are interested in animals, and animal study offers many avenues into important life science concepts, including that animals have basic needs (air, water, food, habitats); that characteristics distinguish one animal from another (coverings, coloring, legs and feet, heads); that young animals inherit characteristics from their parents; that animals grow and change; that animals live in a variety of habitats; and that seasonal changes affect some animals.

Plants should be taught as living things that share characteristics with animals and can be distinguished from nonliving things. Many opportunities for teaching children about plants should be made available. Specific content to be covered includes that plants have basic needs (water, air, light, soil); that the main parts of most plants are roots, stems, and leaves; that plants grow and change; that different plants grow in different environments; and that seasonal changes affect most plants.

Understanding the bodies we inhabit is important to all of us, and kindergartners are certainly interested in learning about their own bodies. Developing knowledge of *the body* as a living organism is key to the life science curriculum in kindergarten. Primary learning elements in this area should include that people are living things; that people take in information about the world through their five senses; that different body parts (including the sense organs) perform different functions; that people change and grow; and that people are alike and different.

Physical science

Physical science for kindergartners should involve them in the exploration of real phenomena that they can experience directly and that relate directly to their lives. This approach does not mean that the learning involved will be anything less than real science. The idea is to provide scientifically valid understandings in forms that fit the cognitive abilities of five- and six-year-olds. For example, in kindergarten, the study of *matter* will involve children in activities (spelled out in Chapter 3) that teach the following content: matter can be divided into solids, liquids, and gasses; matter changes form through melting, freezing, evaporating, and condensing; matter can be classified based on observable physical properties.

Examining the physics of *sound, heat, and light* is appropriate in the new kindergarten science curriculum. It would be logical to tie these explorations to the study of the senses recommended within the life sciences. The core concepts for kindergartners in this area include that vibrating objects produce sound; that the pitch of a sound changes with the speed of vibration; that heat comes from different sources; that heat can move from one object to another; that light comes from different sources; and that light travels in straight lines unless it strikes an object.

Earth and space science

Studying the *weather* provides lots of opportunities to teach science content and processes. The changing weather that most climates offer gives teachers a natural laboratory for studying this part of the earth science curriculum. Basic elements of the weather curriculum include that weather conditions can change from day to day and from season to season; that the four seasons follow a pattern based on elements of weather; and that weather can be observed, described, measured, and predicted.

The surface of our planet is composed of *land and water*, and studying land, water, and how they are related represents important science content. The concepts at the core of an examination of Earth's land and water include that the Earth provides resources people use; that the Earth's surface has many identifiable features (hills, mountains, valleys, oceans, lakes, rivers, streams); that people and nature change the Earth; that nature changes the Earth in slow (erosion, weathering) and fast (earthquakes, landslides, volcanoes) ways.

The sky has been a source of mystery and amazement for as long as people have been looking up, and young children are fascinated by it. While children's abilities to fully comprehend the distances involved and the abstract nature of scientific knowledge about space are limited, they are interested in what they can observe. They can learn essential concepts such as that objects can be seen in the daytime and/or nighttime sky, including the sun, moon, stars, planets, and clouds; that the moon goes through a predictable cycle of phases; that the Earth is part of a solar system of nine planets revolving around the sun.

Science processes

As science content is covered in the new kindergarten, science processes are also taught. Science processes are used throughout instruction in all three areas of the science content curriculum. The emphasis on science processes here is meant to signal the intent that all children develop a sense of themselves as problem solvers with the ability to apply scientific knowledge and processes to the analysis of real problems. Over the course of their early schooling, we want students to internalize a personal model of scientific reasoning that will be useful to them throughout their lives.

Observation is the first element in such a model. As children are learning about their five senses, they should also be learning how to make careful observations using each of those senses. Careful observation means attending closely to the details of what's being examined, paying careful attention to the complexity in what's all around us, and noticing the properties that make one thing distinct from another.

Classification is a scientific process that builds on careful observation. As children are able to attend to details, complexity, and distinguishing properties, they become able to use their observations to make more sophisticated judgments about what objects or phenomena can be grouped together. Both inductive (from specific to general) and deductive (from general to specific) reasoning should be taught as classification lessons are presented. When children study sets of objects and decide which objects are alike and different, they are thinking inductively, starting with individual cases and forming categories into which the individual cases will fit. When they start with categories in mind and examine individual cases to see if they fit their categories, they are thinking deductively. Both kinds of thinking are vital to intellectual development in general and scientific thinking in particular.

Hypothesizing is an important part of scientific thinking. Thinking hypothetically is usually considered too difficult a cognitive task for young children, but we are simply asking children to make good guesses to explain what they observe (e.g., "Why do you think the plant's leaves turned brown?"). The idea is to generate possible explanations that can be checked out using scientific means. If children are unwilling to venture guesses, verifying the accuracy of those guesses will be impossible. I say "good" guesses because I want even young children to have some reasoned (as opposed to random) explanations for why they guess as they do. I don't expect scientifically accurate guesses, but guesses they can explain.

Investigation follows directly from hypothesizing. Here we are helping children set up situations in which their guesses can be assessed as accurate or not. Some investigations involve systematic observation and recording of naturally occurring phenomena (e.g., keeping track of the changes in plants outside the classroom as the seasons change). Others are more like formal scientific experiments in which variables are defined and controlled (e.g., setting up a comparison among plants that get water, light, and soil, those that get water and soil only, and those that get light and soil only). The goal is to help children see that their guesses can be systematically investigated. The point is not to prove children right or wrong, but to teach them how to use science processes to gather useful information that can help solve important problems. It is the responsibility of the teacher to set up investigations in ways that generate scientifically accurate findings. The process is important, but real science content must drive children's investigations.

Interpretation is another high-level cognitive skill that many believe is beyond the capacities of young children. While there may be some limitations in how far they can go, kindergarten-aged students can make general statements about the results of their investigations. The key is to keep it simple while being faithful to scientific principles. Interpretations should grow directly from the hypotheses and investigations (e.g., plants need soil, water, and light to be healthy).

Children should be taught to keep a record of their experiences all along the steps of the scientific process. *Communication* is the process of making such a record. The idea is to show children the importance of keeping track of what they are learning. As they are observing, classifying, hypothesizing, investigating, and interpreting, they should also be drawing, dictating, writing, tallying, graphing, photographing, taping, and talking about what they are doing. Each process will be enhanced as children learn to make careful records that communicate what they have accomplished and how they did it.

Social Studies

The National Council for the Social Studies (NCSS, 1994, p. 1) provides the following definition of social studies:

> *Social studies is the integrated study of the social sciences and humanities to promote civic competence. Within the school program, social studies provides coordinated, systematic study drawing upon such disciplines as anthropology, archaeology, economics, geography, history, law, philosophy, political science, psychology, religion, and sociology.*

Social studies instruction is a vital part of the new kindergarten, and rudimentary (but fundamentally sound) concepts and understandings that promote civic competence are taught in a coordinated, systematic manner. The elements to be systematically introduced in kindergarten are listed in Figure 2–4. These elements have their roots in the social science and humanities

SELF

| shared and unique characteristics
| valuing self and others
| growth and change
| needs versus wants
| feelings

FAMILY

| similarities and differences
| family histories
| roles and responsibilities

COMMUNITY

| rights and responsibilities
| rules and laws
| production, distribution,
  and consumption
| kinds of work
| values, traditions, and customs

Figure 2-4 | Social Studies Curriculum Outline

disciplines and are presented in ways that, in the words of NCSS, "help young people develop the ability to make informed and reasoned decisions for the public good as citizens of a culturally diverse, democratic society in an interdependent world" (1994, p. 1).

I have organized the social studies curriculum using the logic that children's worlds center on themselves and expand out to include their families and communities. The self, family, community structure for addressing important social studies content is appropriate at the kindergarten level. Again, the social studies curriculum is not independent of what is being taught and learned in the other subject areas, but its importance as discrete knowledge that needs to be systematically taught is emphasized. I have heard some kindergarten teachers say, "I teach social studies every time the children clean up, work in centers, or go to lunch." Yes, these teachable moments will always offer opportunities to help children learn to cooperate, share, and get along, but the new kindergarten includes planned instruction that gets at real social studies content and provides a basis for guiding children's development as good citizens in the classroom and beyond.

Self

A primary understanding that all children should acquire is that they are the same as and different from other human beings. Individual children have both *shared and unique characteristics*. We want children to develop a sense of themselves as freestanding, unique individuals who are special because of their differences, but we do them (and our society) a disservice if we fail to help them see how they are *like* other children and all humankind. It is natural to help kindergartners see their shared and unique characteristics as they learn about their bodies, their families, and their communities.

As children are learning to compare themselves to others, they need to learn the importance of *valuing self and others*. That all people, including ourselves, have worth and dignity is one of life's most important lessons. Sometimes, we get so hung up in school on helping children to value themselves (i.e., developing a positive self-concept) that we inadvertently teach them to think others must be somehow inferior. When we put too much focus on helping kids feel unique and special, and forget to emphasize what they have in common with others, we put them at risk of thinking that only children who have characteristics like their own are worthwhile and valuable. At the same time children learn that they have shared and unique characteristics, they should also learn that individuals with different characteristics are special too. Life is not a contest to see who can corner the market on some limited amount of positive self-esteem. Children who learn to value themselves *and* others are way ahead of those whose self-concept is measured in relation to their superiority to real or imaginary peers.

Children are interested in their own *growth and change*, and this is an appropriate component of the kindergarten social studies curriculum. As a kindergarten teacher, I was fascinated with the amount of growth and learning that occurred during the kindergarten year. Children mature rapidly in the physical, social, emotional, and cognitive domains, and they should participate in observing, recording, and investigating their own development. Math and

APPLICATIONS

A primary understanding that all children should acquire is that they are the same as *and* different from other human beings.

Imagine that you are the teacher in a kindergarten that is virtually homogeneous in terms of race, ethnicity, and socioeconomic status. Almost all of the families in your school zone are white, European-American, and lower-middle class. What specific elements would you include in your curriculum to be sure your students develop an understanding of and appreciation for those who are different from the children and families they see every day?

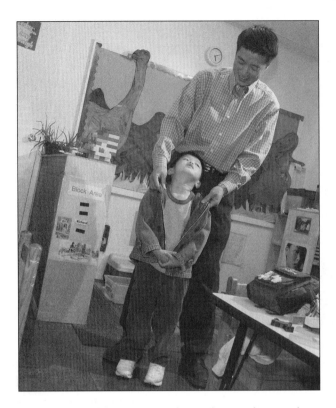

Children's worlds center on themselves and expand out to include their families and communities.

science skills and concepts (e.g., measurement, the body, record keeping) can be applied as children study their own growth and how they are changing.

Understanding the universal need for food, clothing, and shelter is a part of kindergarten social studies, but it is also important for the children be able to deal with the concept of *needs versus wants*. The pattern established above for looking at similarities and differences holds here as well. All humans must satisfy their needs in order to survive, but how those needs are met in different settings is quite different—not better or worse, but different. So the food, clothing, and shelter that all children need will look different depending on factors like place, time, climate, and economic conditions. Similarly, while most people want more than they need to survive, the nature of those wants will look different in different settings. Distinguishing needs from wants is a difficult cognitive activity for young children, especially in a society that has its own difficulties making such a distinction, but an emphasis on universal human needs can make beginning understandings possible.

An exploration of self should include an examination of *feelings*. As a teacher and a parent, I believe that children have a right to their feelings. They don't pick out ways to feel; they just feel. They can learn to recognize their feelings and those of others, but the goal is not for them to be able to decide what feelings are preferable in polite society or desirable for the classroom. Children also need to learn that they cannot express their feelings in ways that violate the rights of others. They have a right to their feelings, but they don't have the right to express their anger (disappointment, joy, or whatever) any way they want. So the big lessons are that you (and everyone else) have feelings; that you can learn to recognize your feelings (and those of others); and that you (and others) can learn to express feelings in ways that don't threaten or disturb those around you.

Family

Families are social institutions in place to meet individual needs. Helping children see the connections between themselves as individuals and the institutions that surround them will be a major thread of the social studies curriculum throughout school. Starting with the family makes sense because it is the first institution kindergartners experience and the one most familiar to them. Exploring *similarities and differences* in the forms and functions of families is important to helping young children understand the place of family in everyone's life, while learning that all families don't have to look like their own to be legitimate. The postmodern family takes many forms, many of which were unknown or invisible just a few generations ago. It is not the role of the teacher to make value judgments (overt or otherwise) about the relative merit of one family structure over another. The idea is that families provide an essential home base for human development, and they need not look the same to accomplish their purposes.

No matter its configuration, every family has a history, and studying *family histories* provides an avenue for exploring many important social science concepts. Looking at family histories helps children see continuity and change, gives them a chance to observe connections across generations, introduces them to the study of history, lets them compare the past with the present, and teaches them that they and all people have cultural roots. The best instruction will connect the child directly to his or her own family history, and kindergarten children will need the help and support of their families to make such connections. The potential benefits of the interactions involved far outweigh the difficulties.

The notion of *roles and responsibilities* is a primary sociological concept that is appropriately introduced within a study of the family. As family forms are explored, it is logical to discuss the roles that make families function well. Children can begin to see the connections between their roles within the family (son/daughter, brother/sister, grandson/granddaughter, etc.) and the overall constellation of family roles. They can also learn that privileges and responsibilities are associated with various roles and begin to see that they have role-based responsibilities that contribute to the overall wellbeing of their families (and the other institutions of which they are a part).

Community

As you can see, the emphasis on social studies in kindergarten is on helping children see connections between their immediate experience and the larger social world. Many of the same principles are emphasized while moving from a focus on the self, through the family, to the community. That children have *rights and responsibilities* is a good example. I teach children that their classroom is a community of learners. In Chapter 4, we will see that it is essential to classroom management that children see themselves as having responsibility for everyone else's learning in the classroom community. In the context of classroom community, the idea is to help children understand that everyone has the right to feel safe and experience conditions that maximize his/her chances to develop and learn. Further, everyone has responsibility for ensuring that everyone else feels safe and able to learn. As children explore communities beyond school (e.g., neighborhoods, towns, cities), the reciprocal nature of rights and responsibilities will continue to be emphasized.

Five- and six-year-olds are just learning about fairness, equity, and justice. They go from thinking of themselves as the center of the universe to developing understandings that others have their own motives and perspectives. They are ready to learn about the place of *rules and laws* in promoting fair and equitable treatment in classroom communities and larger social contexts. Rules are taught as necessary limits that are useful in their lives, rather than as arbitrary constraints imposed by the strong on the weak. Rules are in place to protect individual rights, and all children have the responsibility to follow rules and laws because of the protection that they provide to themselves and others. Even young children can have a hand in creating classroom rules, but the main lesson is that rules have reasonable purposes. We follow rules because they make our lives together better, not to avoid punishment of authority figures acting on arbitrary (or oppressive) standards.

The basic economic concepts of *production, distribution, and consumption* have a place in kindergarten social studies curriculum. Children often have little or no knowledge of how the products they use every day are made and distributed. They may have incomplete or distorted notions of the relationship between being paid to produce goods or services and purchasing the goods and services that workers and their families need. Our economic system is complex and much of it is distant from young children's experience, but they can learn a great deal about how the things they use every day (e.g., food, clothing, books, toys) are produced, distributed, and consumed.

Part of studying economic production includes looking at the *kinds of work* that people do. It is a long-standing tradition in primary school to study "community helpers." It makes good sense for kindergartners to look at the kinds of work that happens around them within a study of their community. I recommend that the usual focus on helpers (e.g., doctors, nurses, firefighters, and police officers) be expanded to include more of the kinds of work that are apparent in the immediate community. The big message is that all work is important and worthy of respect. Work itself is honorable activity, and work provides individuals with personal integrity and the monetary means to participate as consumers in the economic processes that drive much of our society.

Cultural groups have their own *values, traditions, and customs,* and as our society continues to become more culturally diverse, it becomes imperative that children learn to see the beauty in the multicultural world they inhabit. Once again, the emphasis should be on what's the same and what's different. What's the same is that all cultures have ways to meet the needs and concerns of their members. What's different is that there are many ways to address those needs and concerns. As children study how basic needs are met in their immediate communities and in communities in other parts of the world, they can learn about differences in what foods are eaten and how they are prepared, differences in what clothing is worn and why, and differences in where people live and reasons for those differences. The point is not to emphasize differences as oddities, but to encourage an understanding of differences as imminently reasonable ways to accomplish shared ends. The same approach turns examining other cultural elements such as customs, traditions, and celebrations into learning experiences that awaken children to the strength and beauty of our multicultural world.

Health and Physical Education

It's hard to know exactly what to include in a health and physical education curriculum for kindergarten because some of the elements that are important to this subject matter area are addressed in other curriculum areas. For example, the study of the body is an essential piece of the life science curriculum,

and feelings are studied in social studies. Further, elements of movement related to dance could be placed within the arts curriculum. The curriculum
model I am suggesting should be comprehensive in the sense that it gives you a
clear idea of what should be taught in kindergarten. The organization of the
curriculum (i.e., what goes where) is not as important as being sure that what
needs to be there is there somewhere.

Health gets quite a lot of instructional time in kindergarten but physical education instruction is most often left to physical education teachers, when the
school provides them. My position is that physical education (like health) is the
job of the classroom teacher, whether the services of a physical education specialist are available or not. I agree with the position statement from the National Association for Sport and Physical Education (NASPE, 2000) that programs for
young children should be planned and organized by teachers as part of the overall educational program, using both direct and indirect teaching methods. The
connections among physical development, learning, and development in other
domains are too important to be relegated to "whatever kids get at recess" status.

I put health and physical education together because the purpose of both
is to promote healthy living practices in young children. The current generation of children is not a healthy group, and contemporary young adults are not
engaging in healthy eating or physical activity patterns (Torgan, 2002). Learning the importance of health and fitness begins in early childhood. Including
key concepts and understandings as well as developing positive dispositions toward a healthy lifestyle deserve special attention in the new kindergarten curriculum (see Figure 2–5).

Health

A central goal of health instruction in kindergarten is to help children develop
positive *personal health habits*. It is not too early to introduce young children
to the importance of proper handwashing and teeth brushing. They can also

HEALTH	PHYSICAL EDUCATION
personal health habits	body awareness
nutrition	movement
safety	fitness

Figure 2–5 | Health and Physical Education Curriculum Outline

begin to understand the relationship between getting appropriate amounts of sleep, rest, and exercise, and being alert, energetic, and healthy. The approach in kindergarten is to show children direct connections between taking care of their bodies and being happy and healthy. Hygiene and health habits are not taught as abstract concepts to be applied later in life; they are presented as real and meaningful to kids right now.

An emphasis on proper *nutrition* parallels the development of personal health habits. Again, the overarching message is that it is part of children's responsibility to take good care of their bodies, including learning what foods maximize their chances to be healthy now and as they grow and mature. Teaching about the food groups is popular in kindergarten, and this is a good idea as long as children see that the purpose of knowing about food groups is to help them make balanced choices about foods. It's easy to see the natural connections between nutrition content and studies of the body (science) as well as knowledge related to the self and production, distribution, and consumption (social studies). Guiding children's understandings of these connections will go a long way toward improving content coverage across the kindergarten curriculum.

Health instruction includes helping children develop positive personal health habits.

Safety is the third major area in the kindergarten health curriculum. In order for children to remain healthy, they need to learn to follow certain safety rules. This is a good place to bring home the point that rules and laws studied as part of the social studies curriculum have genuine applicability to our everyday lives. Rules regarding safety at home, at school, and in the community should be taught as ways we agree to behave in order to keep everyone healthy and safe. Important lessons include helping children become aware of drug use and abuse, fire prevention measures, procedures for reporting danger and emergencies, and playground safety. It is not our place to teach five- and six-year-olds that they alone are responsible for their own health and safety; but it is our job to show them ways to do what they can to help adults protect and care for them.

Physical education

Like health, the physical education curriculum is closely tied to concepts taught in science and social studies. *Body awareness* means teaching children to become more conscious of their bodies and how they fit into the space around them. At the same time they are learning the parts of the body and how to take care of the health and safety of their bodies, kindergartners should be learning how to control their bodies in space. This begins with becoming aware of their bodies as objects over which they have control.

In my own kindergarten teaching, this apparently obvious lesson was always a challenge. Children are so busy living in their bodies that they have a hard time stepping back from their immediate experience to consider how that living might be consciously controlled. Helping children recognize the dimensions and limits of their bodies, develop balance, and control of their bodies' movements through space are important elements of the kindergarten physical education curriculum.

Movement is sometimes classified with dance as part of the arts curriculum. Here, I want to think of movement as a larger construct that includes, but is not limited to, elements of dance, gymnastics, games, and sport. Learning about movement, improving movement capabilities, and understanding the connections between movement and overall health are what movement instruction in kindergarten should be about. Kindergarteners are undergoing rapid large- and fine-motor skills development. Some children will be able to run, gallop, hop, jump, and skip with fluidity and grace; others will have trouble walking across the room without crashing into the furniture and each other. Some children will have well-developed eye-hand and eye-foot coordination; others will have difficulty throwing, catching, or kicking a ball. Some children will have well-developed fine-motor dexterity and coordination; others will look awkward just picking up a crayon. All children will need opportunities to learn about and practice movement and motor skills. Specific instructional activities designed to develop coordination and dexterity are essential to a balanced kindergarten program.

Teaching *fitness* as a lifetime goal ties directly to the development of personal health habits. Physical activity is essential to healthy living, and children need to develop an understanding of the importance of lifetime fitness and explore ways to be fit in the here and now. Children need to engage in moderate to vigorous physical activity for short periods of time as part of their everyday experience in school. Some of these activities will be planned by the teacher, and some will be student selected during outdoor or indoor play periods. Children should become aware of their bodies' reactions to physical activity (i.e., increased heart rate, breathing, and perspiration), and they should see connections between physical activity and a healthy lifestyle. Body awareness, movement, and fitness should all be closely tied to health instruction. The health

Art and music deserve to be experienced for their own sake.

and physical education curriculum is linked to the other subject-matter areas and to other dimensions of development, making it a vital part of the kindergarten program.

Art and Music

Art and music have a long history as central parts of traditional kindergarten programs. Spontaneous singing and natural opportunities for representing ideas and feelings through artistic expression make kindergarten a fun and interesting place to be. For all but the most diehard advocates for more academics in early childhood, it would be unthinkable to leave art and music experiences out of the kindergarten day. But art and music instruction deserves a place in the organized curriculum for reasons more compelling than because it's fun and has always been there. Current research and theory suggest that children's overall learning and development are strongly influenced by learning and development in the art and music domains. Further, the need to help children understand the value of the arts to well-rounded individuals and societies has never been greater.

What we know about multiple forms of intelligence (Gardner, 1993, 1998) tells us that the development of musical and spatial intelligence is important in all children and critical in some. Early experiences with music and art help children recognize and use special intellectual capabilities that might be unnoticed or undervalued without explicit attention. In addition, current research in the area of brain development indicates that art and music experiences in early childhood positively influence brain function and foster success in other cognitive and academic areas (Davies, 2000; O'Brien, 1999).

Art and music are inherently valuable. They deserve to be experienced for their own sake. A society that diminishes the arts diminishes its humanity. Art and music are afterthoughts in many parts of contemporary culture, and art and music instruction is in jeopardy in our schools. Individuals who do not have the opportunity to learn about and experience the arts miss opportunities to see connections between themselves and others and between one culture and another. The Consortium of National Arts Education Associations identified national standards for arts education, and its report emphasized the importance of helping children see the influence of the arts on their own lives and on the cultures in which they live (CNAEA, 1994). So, including systematic as well as spontaneous art and music instruction in kindergarten is vital to children's development as personal and cultural beings.

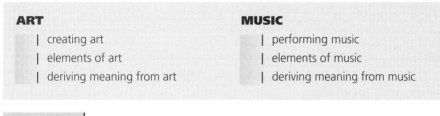

ART	MUSIC
creating art	performing music
elements of art	elements of music
deriving meaning from art	deriving meaning from music

Figure 2–6 | Art and Music Curriculum Outline

Although the overlap between art and music is considerable (as are links to other subject matter areas), I have organized the description of curriculum elements into separate sets. Figure 2–6 outlines these descriptions.

Art

The centerpiece of the kindergarten art curriculum has to be about children *creating art*, that is, expressing their ideas, emotions, and creativity through a variety of art media. One of my disappointments as I visit kindergartens is the relative dearth of genuinely creative opportunities for young children. Most of the "art" that many teachers provide is really craftwork. Children are typically given teacher-prepared materials to color, cut out, and paste together into some prescribed form. The object is to produce a cabin, duck, or whatever that looks as close to the teacher's model as possible. Craftwork activities may be fine for teaching children to follow directions and helping them develop fine-motor skills, but craftwork is not art. Children create art when they produce original forms from their own imagination, memory, and experience. This doesn't mean that they are left to produce art without support and instruction. They need help learning art processes and how to use the tools of art. And they need opportunities to learn about the properties and artistic potential of a wide variety of media and art forms, including collage, drawing, painting, printmaking, fiber art, mixed media, and modeling. We want children to have experiences in school that lead them to the perception that they are artists and that art is a valuable part of their lives.

Part of developing personal artistic technique and learning to appreciate the art of others involves learning about the basic *elements of art*. Color, line, texture, shape, and space are art elements that kindergartners can learn about and use in their own creations. It may seem pedantic to "teach" elements of art to young children, but lots of evidence, especially examples of children's art produced at the Reggio Emilia preschools in Italy (Edwards, Gandini, & Forman, 1993) suggests that creativity is enhanced by such instruction. As we look closely at kindergarten instruction in Chapter 3, we will explore spontaneous and systematic ways to teach content like elements of art.

Art should be taught as personal expression, symbolic communication, and cultural creation. *Deriving meaning from art* should have a prominent place in children's school experience. As children learn to express their individual creativity, they should also be learning about the power of the art of others to communicate feelings and ideas. In the same ways authors and illustrators are highlighted during literacy instruction, so should artists be recognized and their work valued as part of art (and music) experiences. Exploring examples of a variety of art forms helps children recognize how artists use the elements of art to create balance, unity, and mood. Further, children can begin to interpret, critique, and appreciate art from their own perspectives. In addition, children can begin to understand that art is a vehicle for the expression and transmission of culture. As they study art produced in other cultures and in the past, they learn something about others and themselves. We want children to come away from their experiences with art having an increased awareness of the art all around them, an appreciation for the art of a variety of cultures, and the strong sense that art has an important place in their own lives.

Music

The organization of the music curriculum parallels that of art. *Performing music*, that is, singing and playing musical instruments, has the same status as creating art. It would be silly to teach young children about music but not have them make it. As in art, we want children to see themselves as musicians and to see the place of music in a full, well-rounded life. Children need opportunities to perform a varied repertoire of music. They should be singing daily and performing on musical instruments regularly. They can learn to reproduce newly heard melodies in their singing and new patterns with their rhythm instruments. Music should be woven throughout the fabric of the day, and children should be experiencing opportunities to make music spontaneously, often creating their own rhythms, tunes, and lyrics, and in more structured ways during organized music times. Connections between literacy learning, movement, and art should be capitalized on as music is performed, but young children's love of music should be nurtured and valued as a vehicle for self-expression and intrinsic reward.

Studying the *elements of music* can enhance children's understanding and appreciation. Musical elements that kindergartners ought to be exposed to include rhythm (steady beat and repeating patterns), pitch (high and low), volume (loud and soft), and tempo (slow and fast). Learning about these elements in the context of singing and playing will enhance children's awareness of what makes music music and improve their capacities for making music musical.

Like all the arts, music has personal and cultural dimensions, and *deriving meaning from music* is important in both. We want children to see music as a personally fulfilling opportunity to express emotions, feelings, and ideas. We can also help children begin to understand music as a communication system with its own forms of symbolic representation that work along with special text that is often written in a poetic format. The words to songs can be written as well as sung, and opportunities to connect reading and writing with music abound. Cultural meaning is also conveyed through music. Kindergartners can learn to identify musical styles and even musical instruments associated with different cultural groups. They should experience listening to and studying a wide variety of contemporary and historical musical forms. Listening for similarities and differences across time, cultures, and genres is important intellectual activity that develops appreciation for music as an art form and a cultural artifact.

Closing Thoughts

This chapter is all about curriculum. The attempt has been to provide an example of a kindergarten curriculum in enough detail that novice teachers can get a good idea of what kinds of content make sense for contemporary kindergartners. The example also serves as a tool with which experienced teachers and supervisors can assess the substance in their current kindergarten programs. As I said in the introduction, this is not meant to be *the* curriculum, but it does provide a model of what's possible for kindergarten programs today.

I believe that defining what should be taught—having an explicit, written curriculum—is an essential element of successful contemporary kindergarten programs. Two common alternatives are not satisfactory. The first, substituting standards for curriculum, means that teachers focus too much time and energy on a narrow set of measurable competencies that leave out more than they cover. The second, acting as if the provision of certain kinds of activities equals curriculum, leaves to chance children's opportunities to learn real content and develop real skills. The kindergarten curriculum ought to have depth, breadth, and integrity. It should include those academic elements that are typically measured by standards-based accountability models, but it should cover much more intellectual territory and allow much more learning to occur. The kindergarten curriculum ought to spell out the substance kindergartners should be learning, and it should appear in a form that allows teachers to see clear distinctions between what is to be taught and how to teach it.

This book intentionally separates curriculum from instruction in ways that are sometimes hard to find in early childhood curriculum texts. While they claim to be about curriculum, many of these books focus on describing ways to set up classrooms and organize activities for young children. It's as if activities and curriculum are the same thing. The logic in this book is plain and simple. The curriculum is what we should be teaching. Instruction is the many ways the curriculum can be taught. This chapter described what to teach in the new kindergarten. The following chapter is all about ways to teach it.

FOR YOUR CONSIDERATION

1. What is the place (if any) of contemporary kindergarten as a buffer between home and "real" school?

2. What are the advantages and disadvantages of the increasing emphasis on content in relation to process in the kindergarten curriculum?

3. What distinctions can be made among curricula, standards, and objectives?

4. What arguments can be made for and against teaching reading in kindergarten?

5. What are potentially positive and negative consequences for children of moving real subject matter to the center of the kindergarten curriculum?

LEARNING ACTIVITIES

INDIVIDUAL ACTIVITIES

- Interview an elementary school principal or kindergarten supervisor about the kindergarten curriculum. Ask to see the published materials supplied to kindergarten teachers under their supervision, and try to find out school and district expectations for implementing the prescribed curriculum and using the materials supplied.

- Search the Internet for standards from professional organizations in each subject area of the kindergarten curriculum. Find out which organizations have standards explicitly for kindergarten, and examine the curriculum elements in this chapter in relation to those standards.

SMALL GROUP ACTIVITIES

- Reflect on the science and social studies instruction your group has observed in kindergarten classrooms. Use the curriculum outlines in this chapter to gauge how much of the science and social studies curriculum described is being taught in the kindergartens observed. Discuss why the curriculum content is or is not being taught.

- Plan a presentation that could be made at an information night for parents of new kindergartners. The purpose of the presentation is to share your kindergarten curriculum with parents. In your plan, decide what to cover, how you'll organize what you'll present, and exactly what you'll say.

LARGE GROUP ACTIVITIES

- Assign a different state to each class member and have everyone locate and download kindergarten curriculum materials from departments of education Web sites for their assigned states. In class, form groups based on subject matter areas and compare format, organization, and content across states.

- Lead a discussion of the place of reading instruction in kindergarten. Address issues such as: Should children learn to read in kindergarten? Should a phonics-based approach dominate reading instruction? Should reading instruction receive more time than other subjects in the kindergarten day? Should progression to first grade be based on kindergartners' reading abilities?

CHAPTER | 3

How Do I Teach in the New Kindergarten?

KEY TERMS AND CONCEPTS

Problem solving model

Continuum of teaching strategies

Incidental teaching strategies

• Scaffolding

• Zone of proximal development

Thematic teaching

• Units

• Projects

• Integrated theme studies

Tactical teaching

• Grouping

• Modeling and Demonstrating

• Coaching

• Tutoring

• Discussing

• Practicing

• Individualizing

Direct teaching strategies

K nowing what to teach is not the same as knowing how to teach it. My view is that too many preservice teachers are not fully prepared to design and run kindergarten programs. They don't have a clear idea of what the kindergarten curriculum ought to include or a strong sense of how to teach in ways that ensure that the content of that curriculum is learned by children. The approach in many early childhood teacher education programs has been to teach a lot about child development and a lot about how to set up classrooms in ways that allow children to construct their own understandings. This knowledge is important, but almost all of these teachers will be working in public schools with prescribed curricula and accountability expectations they are required to meet.

Successful teaching requires different kinds of instructional approaches and strategies.

New teachers trained with an exclusive focus on developmental approaches are often lost when it comes to meeting the expectations of their jobs. Some university instructors condemn public school kindergartens as "developmentally inappropriate." Instead of adjusting their university-based instruction to address the changing pressures on teachers, they demean classroom teachers who implement anything other than constructivist approaches. This places new teachers between a rock and a hard place when they start teaching in the real world.

In Chapter 2, I described a complete kindergarten curriculum. Knowing what needs to be taught is necessary but not sufficient by itself. The curriculum includes different kinds of knowledge and skills, and successful teaching requires that teachers have different kinds of instructional approaches and strategies. I believe there is an important place for child development knowledge and constructivist approaches, but these should be learned alongside a variety of perspectives on how children learn and the best ways to teach them. This makes learning to be a teacher much more difficult, but it gives new teachers tools they need to successfully navigate the complex waters of public school settings.

This chapter is all about how to teach. It doesn't include everything a competent teacher needs to know about teaching, but it does provide essential information that beginning kindergarten teachers need in order to meet public school expectations. I do not prescribe a finite set of teaching strategies that can be applied in any setting. Teachers, like other professionals, process information from a variety of sources and make decisions based on their own best judgment. Good teaching is good decision making that leads to good problem solving. The goal in this chapter is to provide enough insight into instructional options so that teachers can make good decisions and good teaching can happen.

In the first section of this chapter, I discuss the essential responsibility of teachers to be professional problem solvers who exercise their knowledge of teaching to maximize the learning opportunities of their students. I argue that teachers (not legislators, program developers, or administrators) are in the best position to make the day-to-day decisions necessary to ensure every student's success. Next, I present a continuum of teaching strategies as a guide for instructional decision making. In this section, I take seriously the argument that content should be taught in different ways, to different students, in different schools, in different communities. The continuum is designed to help new teachers decide what will work best in their particular circumstances. In the next section, I build on the ideas in the continuum and provide examples of different ways to teach different elements of the curriculum. I conclude the chapter with a discussion of what it means to do everything possible to help each child develop into a confident, happy, healthy individual who is also academically successful.

Teacher as Professional Problem Solver

Throughout my career as a teacher and teacher educator, I have argued that teachers are the most important ingredient for educational success and that they should be given more power, more responsibility, and more credit for making schools better. Almost everyone seems to agree with the first part—that teachers make the most difference—but few are willing to buy into the more important, second part—giving teachers power, responsibility, and credit. It's ironic that teachers are acknowledged to be the most important variable in the education equation, but that someone else must be responsible for telling them what to do and how to do it. The result is teacher-proof curricula, scripted teaching programs, and an accountability movement that narrows the curriculum and undermines teacher autonomy (Hatch 2002).

To justify giving real power to teachers, we must be able to make the case that teachers are front-line experts who are able to process the complex information available to them (and no one else), then make good decisions about what's best for their students. They must take on the role of professional problem solvers. I see effective kindergarten teachers as those who possess the knowledge, intelligence, and analytic ability to systematically study the settings in which they work, to know the strengths and needs of their students, families, and communities, to understand the constraints and supports of the systems around them, to make sound decisions based on an examination of a variety of options, and to monitor the results of those decisions and adjust accordingly. No one knows the immediate experience of teaching better than teachers. No one is in a position to know more about children, families, and communities than teachers. No one knows what it's like to teach in particular schools, with particular administrators and particular norms and expectations better than teachers. No one should know better than teachers the most effective ways to deal with the complex issues of teaching and learning. In short, no one is in a better position than teachers to make the on-the-ground decisions required to provide high-quality experiences for kindergarten children.

In the area of professional problem solving, I agree with the general direction advocated by the National Association for the Education of Young Children (NAEYC) in the 1997 version of *Developmentally Appropriate Practices in Early Childhood Programs* (DAP) (Bredekamp & Copple, 1997). NAEYC argues that appropriate practices result from professionals making decisions based on knowledge of "human development and learning, individual characteristics and experiences, and social and cultural contexts" (p. 9). That framework parallels my own, given that my understanding of what constitutes knowledge of human development and learning may be somewhat broader than that reflected in the rest of the DAP document. The important point in both models is that teachers are moved from being technicians implementing someone else's ideas to the status of professional decision makers who take responsibility for applying specialized knowledge and skill to solve real classroom problems.

I work in a teacher preparation program that has as one of its specific objects to help new teachers utilize a professional **problem solving model** (Phillips & Hatch, 2000b). We use case-based teaching in our program to give students opportunities to deal with problems like the ones they will confront in real classrooms (Rand, 2000; Wassermann, 1993). We usually present a well-developed case describing some teaching dilemma or issue drawn from real experience. Students study the scenario ahead of time, then we process the case in class, modeling the kind of problem-solving processes we hope they will internalize and use in their professional practice. Of course, each individual will develop his/her own set of problem-solving strategies, but key elements will be present in any effective model. The essential steps we try to teach include:

1. Pull together what you know.
2. Analyze the situation from a variety of perspectives.
3. Identify the problem(s).
4. Brainstorm a variety of possible solutions (short- and long-term).
5. Anticipate the consequences of each viable option.
6. Make a plan.
7. Take action.
8. Assess the effectiveness of your actions.

I will briefly explain these steps because such a model will be useful in guiding the problem solving development of prospective kindergarten teachers (a detailed example of applying the model is included in the final section of Chapter 4). We ask students to pull together what they know because people have a natural tendency when facing tough problems in schools (and elsewhere) to look for solutions before they really understand the problem. We ask students to write down what they know about the principle players in the scenario (teachers, students, parents, administrators, and others) and about the context (classroom, school, system, community). What they know means just the facts, not interpretations or inferences drawn from the written scenario.

We next try to get students to look at the situation from a variety of perspectives. We ask questions like, "How would a parent describe what's going on here?" or "What do you think the child was thinking when this happened?" or "What would the district supervisor say about this situation?" The idea is to help prospective teachers see that every problem can be looked at in a variety of ways.

How the problem gets defined is critical to successful solutions. Again, how you identify problems will be different depending on where you are standing. Our approach is to look for problems over which teachers have some control. We want teachers to feel responsible for making classrooms better, and to look at dimensions over which they have an influence when they begin defining problems. This is the opposite of throwing up their hands and saying there's nothing they can do because the problems are outside their control (they're caused by the system, parents, community, poverty, etc.). If the case is a good one, it reflects the complexity of real classroom issues, and more than one problem or multilayered problems are evident.

Once problems are identified, we want students to examine a variety of options for seeking solutions. We brainstorm as a group, accepting everyone's suggestions for dealing with the issues at hand. It's tempting to say, "Okay, here's the problem, so this must be the solution." We find it's better to generate as

APPLICATIONS

How the problem gets defined is critical to successful solutions.

Imagine a boy in your kindergarten who seems unable to stay with a task for more than a few seconds. He has trouble attending during large group experiences, and he moves from activity to activity during center time, rarely completing anything. Many teachers start defining potential problems in situations like this by looking at what might be wrong within the child or his home life, but defining problems in terms of elements that *you* can control increases your chances of finding solutions that work. As a starting place for defining this situation, list all the things under your control that might be contributing to the behavior you observe.

many possible solutions as possible, then to analyze each suggestion and look at the probable consequences of its implementation. During this phase, we ask students to revisit the work they did earlier when they looked at the facts and different perspectives. Some solutions are just not viable, some cause as many problems as they solve, and some have unintended consequences but are still worth pursuing. It's almost always the case that there are short-term actions that need to be undertaken immediately and long-term solutions that need to be implemented to make more fundamental changes. This leads us naturally to make an action plan for short- and long-term change. Of course, doing case studies on campus does not allow us to actually take action then assess the results of our actions, but we teach these as critical problem solving steps.

Stepping back from the immediate stress of facing classroom problems is difficult, but being thoughtful, systematic, and knowledgeable in dealing with the issues of teaching is what distinguishes teachers as professionals. Another claim to professional status is related to having specialized knowledge that ordinary individuals don't possess. Professional problem solvers have knowledge, skills, dispositions, and commitments that separate them from others who may also care about children. Solving instructional problems means applying those specialized professional understandings to maximize children's learning. Obviously, knowing the curriculum is essential—if you don't know what children need to learn, how can you ever hope to teach it? Knowing your students and the contexts in which they live is also important to the instructional equation, and knowing yourself as a person and teacher is another key ingredient. However, it's conceivable that someone could know the curriculum, have a solid understanding of his/her students, their families, and their communities, and have a well-developed awareness of his/her own strengths and weaknesses—and still have insufficient understanding of ways to teach. The next section is designed to provide a framework for improving that understanding.

A Continuum of Teaching Strategies

During the heyday of the whole language approach to literacy development (the 1980s and early 1990s), I had the opportunity to teach a class to 1,300 teachers using distance learning technologies. My goal was to help teachers do a better job of teaching young children to read and write by applying principles of the whole language philosophy. My general approach was to value what teachers were already doing, invite them to examine alternative instructional approaches, then make their own decisions about best ways to teach in their individual classrooms. As part of that year-long effort, I developed a **continuum of teaching strategies** that stretched across a range of instructional possibilities (from whole language to phonics-based approaches) (Hatch, 1992). The thinking behind that continuum is still useful as I try to encourage balanced approaches to solving instructional problems in all areas of the curriculum. A modified version of the original continuum is reproduced in Figure 3–1.

Incidental teaching

I'm not crazy about the term "incidental" if it is taken to mean random or serendipitous. **Incidental teaching** does not depend on chance or good fortune; it is a matter of setting up, then taking advantage of teachable moments. These teachable moments are the incidents that make this kind of teaching incidental. Incidental teaching most often takes place one-on-one between teacher and student, but it can happen between teachers and small groups or among students themselves. The learner is typically engaged in a task that is

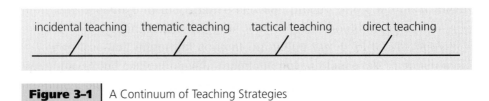

Figure 3-1 | A Continuum of Teaching Strategies

just beyond what he/she can do independently, and the teacher (or more knowledgeable peer) supplies the support, or **scaffolding,** necessary to help the learner accomplish the task. This model is a direct application of the **zone of proximal development** (ZPD) described in the work of Lev Vygotsky (see Chapter 1). Vygotsky's notion was that the most effective instruction happens when adults or more able peers support learning in a zone just above what children can accomplish on their own. What the child can do with assistance today, he/she will be able to do independently tomorrow (Vygotsky, 1978; Berk & Winsler, 1995). As we will see later in this chapter, it is possible to use Vygotsky's ZPD concept at other places along the instructional continuum, but the one-on-one nature of incidental teaching makes this the most logical place to apply it.

I said that incidents for teaching are "set up" and that students are given tasks just beyond their level of independent functioning. That means teachers are not just hovering about hoping for a teachable moment to arise, and children are not just exploring materials or experimenting without purpose. To maximize the effectiveness of incidental teaching, kindergarten teachers need to design activities for their students that engage the students in accomplishing some end. The content of activities can range across the curriculum spectrum from creating art to counting sets of objects. Activities can take the form of games, assignments, or projects, and they can be organized as parts of learning centers, individualized learning packets, or group assignments.

Teachers plan activities so that children will confront tasks just beyond what they can do alone. Kindergarten teachers do not have the time to plan separate activities for each child in their room, so the best activities have outcomes at various levels. This is fairly straightforward if, for example, the content is creating art using modeling clay. Some kindergartners will be just learning to manipulate the medium, while others are ready to represent real objects, and incidental teaching will mean scaffolding the child's efforts to move to the next level of art development. If the content is counting objects in a set, some children will likely be ready to count scores of objects, while others are just learning one-to-one correspondence. Both need help to move to the next level of math understanding, so activities need to be designed in ways that go beyond having the "advanced" child practice doing what he/she can already do or frustrating the child who is not ready to count beyond 10.

Designing such activities requires knowledge of the curriculum and of each child's ZPD. A kindergarten curriculum was described in Chapter 2, and assessment practices are detailed in Chapter 4. For now, it is sufficient to understand that setting up incidental teaching opportunities means developing activities that require children to perform tasks just beyond their level of independent functioning. While there will be times when you will develop unique activities for individual children, the mode will be to design activities that make it possible for children to perform at a variety of levels.

Scaffolding

The efficacy of incidental teaching depends on the effectiveness of teachers' efforts to help students learn what they don't already know. Setting up the teachable moment means nothing unless the teaching part happens. In *How People Learn*, the National Research Council's Committee on Development in the Science of Learning summarized the role of adults in scaffolding children's learning:

> *Adults help make connections between new situations and familiar ones for children. Children's curiosity and persistence are supported by adults who direct their attention, structure their experiences, support their learning attempts, and regulate the complexity and difficulty levels of information for them. (Bransford, Brown, & Cocking, 1999, p. 100)*

Berk and Winsler (1995) have synthesized research and theory in this area. The elements of scaffolding they identify provide a useful framework for thinking about how to use scaffolding during incidental teaching (pp. 26–32):

- joint problem solving
- intersubjectivity
- warmth and responsiveness
- keeping the child in the ZPD
- promoting self-regulation

Each element is discussed below in relation to incidental teaching in kindergarten.

Joint problem solving means that children are engaged with an adult or older child in a collaborative effort to solve a meaningful problem. Vygotsky argued that all learning is social in nature, so social interactions between those who already know something and those who are trying to learn it are the mechanism that makes learning happen. Joint problem solving cannot happen in the absence of a task, and both participants need to be actively engaged in the accomplishment of that task. In kindergarten, this is simply the teacher (or more knowledgeable child) working directly with the child in order to solve the problem built into the task. The subtext of the social interactions of scaffolding is, "I know how to do this. Let's work on it together so you can learn how to do it too."

Intersubjectivity means coming to a shared view of a situation. In scaffolding, it is the process of social negotiation through which the child and teacher arrive at a mutual understanding of the task at hand. Until and unless the teacher and child have the same definition of the situation, learning will be difficult. Intersubjectivity involves two-way communication, and adults have to tune in to the perspectives children bring to the task and adjust their side of the interactions in order for children to move forward. Intersubjectivity is an important ingredient in all positive social interactions, but it is key to effective incidental teaching. Reaching intersubjectivity around the tasks of kindergarten is about sensitive face-to-face interactions between teacher and child, the message to the child being, "I want to understand how you think about this so that together we can figure out the best way to do it."

Warmth and responsiveness is the third ingredient in effective scaffolding. One of the reasons I loved teaching kindergarten—and still love to spend time working with kindergartners—is that it's an important part of my role to express my affection for children. It's not just fun, heart-warming, and self-fulfilling to express love for children; it's good pedagogy. In this case, it's a critical part of sound incidental teaching. In scaffolding situations, children learn best when they feel safe and supported. When interactions are warm, pleasant, and responsive, children will be much more likely to engage fully in the task at hand and much more willing to accept the challenges of work that is by definition beyond what they can do on their own. The message we want to send children here is, "I care about you, I believe you can accomplish this task, and I am here to support your efforts to do so."

Keeping the child in the ZPD is also important to the scaffolding process. There are, of course, tasks that are beyond what the child can do even with adult support. These are outside the zone of proximal development, and no amount of scaffolding will help children accomplish them. While this seems self-evident, I see too many teachers trying to teach content (often because the system requires them to do so) that is clearly above some of their children's zones of proximal development. At the lower end of the ZPD, it is a poor strategy to spend time scaffolding tasks that children can already accomplish on their own. Since each child's ZPD is constantly changing, teachers must monitor these changes and adjust the tasks that children are assigned and the level of scaffolding they provide. A simple rule of thumb can guide teachers' adjustments: "Provide assistance when children need help, and reduce the amount

APPLICATIONS

Our message to children as we work with them is, "What you can do with my help today, you will be doing on your own tomorrow."

Imagine a student who is one of the last in your kindergarten to recognize her name in writing. Make a written plan that shows the anticipated steps you will take to scaffold her learning so she can find the card with her name on it when shown a set of cards with her classmates' names.

of assistance as children's competence increases" (Berk & Winsler, 1995, p. 29). Incidental teaching in kindergarten ought to be targeted to children's zones of proximal development. Our message to children as we work with them is, "What you can do with my help today, you will be doing on your own tomorrow."

Promoting self-regulation means giving children increasing responsibility for regulating the joint activity that defines the scaffolding process. The lessons involved here go beyond accomplishing the immediate task. We want to help children see themselves as having control over their own learning and behavior. In the scaffolding situation, this means gradually giving children more responsibility, while the teacher takes less. One way of promoting self-regulation is to change the nature of the assistance given, for example moving from directives such as, "Let's put all the red ones together" to questions like, "What are some other ways we could group them?" Another is to give children more responsibility for directing the problem solving process itself, so statements like, "Now, let's find all the words that start with p" become questions like, "What do you think we should do next?" The message below the surface of our efforts to promote self-regulation is, "You are a learner, and you are increasing your ability to control what and how you learn."

Incidental teaching is not synonymous with scaffolding; it can be done in much more directed ways. And scaffolding can be done with other instructional approaches along the teaching continuum. But scaffolding is an excellent way to take advantage of teachable incidents in the kindergarten classroom. Scaffolding done well provides a way to accelerate children's development and academic achievement, help children become and see themselves as capable learners, and provide opportunities for teachers to work face-to-face with children in warm, supportive, and learning-filled situations.

Thematic teaching

Organizing instruction around themes has a long history in early childhood classrooms. Many teachers have been trained to use **thematic teaching** as the principal instructional strategy for kindergarten, and integrated theme studies are widely considered to be developmentally appropriate means for packaging learning experiences for young children. My own college teaching once emphasized thematic teaching as the best way to help children learn in kindergarten. However, as my perspective on kindergarten changed to advocating a more balanced approach, I have come to see thematic teaching as powerful and important, but not the only (or even the major) vehicle for carrying the instructional load in the new kindergarten.

Teachers use many instructional approaches that might be called thematic. Some teachers plan **units** by creating series of lessons around an overarching instructional goal. So children studying a social studies unit on roles and responsibilities, for example, might experience one lesson per day over a week-long period that would add to their knowledge of what roles and responsibilities are and how they fit into their experiences as family and classroom members.

Other teachers use **projects** as tools for helping children learn. Projects, as described by Katz and her colleagues (Helm & Katz, 2001; Katz & Chard, 1989), are in-depth investigations of topics of interest to students. Children take an active role in deciding what they want to learn, how they will learn it, and how they will know they have learned it. So a kindergarten class might choose to investigate shoes, decide what they want to learn about shoes, study how shoes are made, plan a visit to a shoe factory, set up a shoe store in their classroom, and create a video explaining the shoe making process to others.

Integrated theme studies are perhaps the most common thematic approach used in kindergarten classrooms. The idea is to organize all or most classroom experiences for a period of time (often a week) around a centralizing theme. The goal is to integrate content learning within a meaningful study of some organizing topic. So teachers may declare next week to be frog week, and children will read about frogs, classify frogs, sing frog songs, write frog stories, count frogs, take a field trip to search for frogs, draw frogs, and so on.

While these approaches are different in many respects, they are all thematic; that is, they organize instruction around an identifiable topic. They each provide conceptual glue that holds the separate pieces of content together into a distinguishable whole. This characteristic is valuable in the classroom because young children have difficulty seeing how fragmented skills and isolated concepts fit together when they are taught separately and outside any meaningful context (IRA/NAEYC, 1998). Thematic teaching deserves a place on a continuum of teaching approaches for kindergarten. It provides ways to help children learn essential content as well as generates opportunities for teaching lessons that go beyond the written-down curriculum.

In the following sections, I describe each kind of thematic teaching, discussing the strengths and weaknesses of each. I describe archetypes in order to make the distinguishing characteristics clear, but teachers should mix and match these and other instructional approaches as they create programs that make sense in their own settings. Ways to do that are discussed later in this chapter.

Units

Units are more linear than integrated. Units are organized to present a series of lessons that build a set of competencies and understandings. Children know they are doing a unit within some specific domain of the curriculum (e.g., a science unit on parts of the body); they know that they will be having instructional experiences related to the unit over a prescribed period of time (e.g., during health period for the next week); and they know that certain skills and concepts will be taught as part of the unit (e.g., identifying the parts of the body). Lessons are sequenced to build information from simple to more complex, and teachers show children connections as lessons progress. The kinds of instructional experiences can vary from direct teaching lessons to more open-ended activities, but all are tied to teaching the specific goals and objectives of the unit.

The major strength of units is that content is presented in a systematic sequence that helps children see the logic of how knowledge is organized. So, for example, they may be learning how scientific information is structured while they are learning about specific body parts. Units are also an interesting and efficient way to organize instruction. Young children enjoy learning real content in an organized way, and units offer relatively easy means for fitting curriculum content into meaningful instructional packages. Problems occur when teachers teach the parts of the unit as separate, disconnected pieces. When this happens, learning the specific content is more difficult, and the benefits of seeing a meaningful whole or understanding how the parts fit together are lost.

Projects

The projects I described here are based on the project approach as presented by Katz and Chard (1989) and Helm and Katz (2001). Projects differ from units in a number of ways. Units consist of lessons and activities that are preplanned by the teacher. The teacher determines the content, plans the lessons, and leads the instruction. In projects, students are given a much larger role in making decisions about what to study and how to study it. They usually select the topic, identify questions they want to answer, design and conduct investigations, and share their findings with others. Projects involve much more child initiation and student decision making than units (Helm & Katz, 2001). Further, projects focus on a topic that children find worthy of investigation, rather than a segment of curriculum.

With projects, children spend long periods of time investigating phenomena like shadows or fire trucks. They have opportunities to learn skills and concepts from the curriculum in their investigations, but the focus is on the topic, and curriculum content is used at the application level to help them process information about that topic. Teachers guide children as project plans are developed and implemented. The key elements of projects are investigations, constructions, and dramatic play (Katz & Chard, 1989). The logic is that children investigate a topic through a variety of direct (field trips and visitors) and indirect (books, videos, photos) experiences; they construct replicas or models of objects or scenes related to their topic; and they use their constructions in their dramatic play to extend and deepen their understanding of the topic at hand. Projects can be used to organize virtually all of the kindergarten day, or

Children investigate project topics through a variety of direct and indirect experiences.

APPLICATIONS

Projects focus on a topic that children find worthy of investigation.

Imagine that you want to try a project with a group of kindergartners who have never done project work before. How will you help the children decide on a project that is worthy of their investigation? What processes will you use to provide them with opportunities to explore potential topics? How will you know when they have selected an appropriate topic?

they can be implemented alongside other approaches (as is recommended in this book).

The project approach is rooted in the British Infant School and Reggio Emilia philosophies (Helm & Katz, 2001). Both philosophies emphasize elements that highlight major advantages of using projects in classrooms, including seeing children as protagonists, collaborators, and communicators (see Chapter 1). As protagonists, children take an active role in their own learning; as collaborators, they work in partnership with teachers, other adults, and other children; and as communicators, they find ways to represent what they are learning in forms that are unique and expressive. Being engaged in projects gives kindergartners opportunities to apply the skills they are learning within the written curriculum to accomplish meaningful tasks. And children are developing habits of mind such as dispositions to "make sense of experience, find things out, persist in seeking solutions to problems, strive for accuracy, and theorize, analyze, hypothesize, and synthesize" (Helm & Katz, 2001, p. 4).

The major drawback of projects is that they are inefficient. Planning and doing projects with children takes a great deal of time, and giving children the power to study what they are interested in can make it difficult to build in the curriculum content that is required in most kindergarten settings. Strategies for "having it both ways" are presented later in this chapter.

Integrated theme studies

Integrated theme studies are ways to organize the instructional activities of a period of time around a theme. While theme studies do not have to include all of the activities for a given period, integrating as much of the curriculum as possible around the theme is usually the goal. Integrated theme studies fall somewhere between units and projects on the dimensions of child initiation and student problem solving. Children's interests are taken into account as themes are chosen, and students usually have choices within certain activities or time periods. But teachers select most of the content, design most of the activities, and orchestrate most of the action.

Teachers who use theme studies as their primary teaching strategy set up their classrooms so that students know what the theme of the week is. If the theme is the beach, then the room is decorated with beach scenes, centers include pictures and objects related to the beach, and books about the beach are prominently displayed. All, or as many as possible, of the school activities for that week are linked to the beach. Student lessons in math, reading, science, social studies, physical education, and art are integrated around the beach theme.

The notion is that young children learn best when concepts and skills are taught in a meaningful context, and the themes provide that context. Planning integrated theme studies means teachers start by brainstorming as many activities as possible related to the theme. Potential activities are examined, altered, eliminated, and added to, based on how well they address kindergarten curriculum elements; then they are organized onto a week's schedule. Theme studies are almost always introduced with an engaging opening activity and brought to closure with some kind of culminating experience.

Using integrated theme studies makes kindergarten an interesting place for children and teachers. Integrating learning experiences across subject areas shows children that the knowledge and skills they are learning have real connections to each other and to the world beyond the classroom. In addition, theme studies offer opportunities for children to learn information, skills, and attitudes that they would not have in a classroom organized to cover the curriculum one subject at a time.

A concern that critics have historically lodged against integrated theme studies is that not enough substance is taught; that is, there is too much emphasis on providing "fun" or "cute" activities and not enough on teaching children what they need to be learning. This concern is justified when the curriculum is an afterthought (or invisible) as theme studies are planned.

For teachers, a major disadvantage is the amount of time and energy required for planning and preparation. Thinking of or finding interesting activities that address significant content is much harder than following the prescribed lessons in textbooks. Setting up classrooms so that a special atmosphere is created each week is much harder than keeping the room the same. And finding books, objects, and materials related to a particular theme is much harder than using whatever the district provides. We deal with these concerns later in the context of making sound decisions by exploring options across the continuum of teaching approaches.

Tactical teaching

Tactical teaching is the term I use to identify a set of approaches that teachers use to accomplish situational objectives in their classrooms. "Tactical" indicates a planned reaction to changing conditions. So tactical teaching is teaching that is planned in reaction to changing conditions in the classroom. It is teaching tailored to the needs of whole classes, of small groups, or of individual students. It is teaching designed to deliver specific content to specific individuals in specific ways. While incidental teaching has the potential to influence all kinds of teaching activities, and thematic teaching involves an overarching approach to organizing instruction, tactical teaching is reactive in the sense that teachers design specific responses to changing needs in the classroom.

As professional problem solvers, teachers need overall strategies for dealing with the larger problems that define teaching (e.g., helping children develop a disposition to love learning while preparing them to pass the end of kindergarten assessment). For me, the teaching strategies described in this chapter provide a framework for making decisions about these larger instructional issues. But a great deal of problem solving happens during the day-to-day experience of running a classroom. Teachers need to be able to use the problem solving model to react to changes in the classroom that could not be anticipated as decisions at the strategy level were undertaken. They need to be able to select from a variety of options in order to generate good solutions to imminent classroom problems. They need a set of reliable tactics that they can employ to accomplish immediate teaching objectives. This doesn't mean that teachers abandon their overall strategies. They can use the tactics described here alongside the elements of incidental, thematic, and direct teaching. These tactics represent tools for adjusting to individual and group needs.

Let's look at some examples:

- The school system's end-of-year assessment requires your kindergartners to demonstrate that they can match upper- to lowercase letters. Your children have been learning about letters all year and have had some experience matching letters, but you want to prepare them to do well on the assessment. The whole class needs special instruction to be sure students are up to speed on matching upper- and lowercase letters.

- You notice that four or five children seem lost when it comes to grasping the addition concept. Most of the other children appear to have the general idea, but these few don't have a clue. They need special attention to help them understand what addition is all about.

- Several weeks into the term, it becomes clear that one of your students is not adjusting to the classroom routines that seem to be working for everyone else. His behavior is not disruptive, but you can see he is not engaged in the learning activities you have planned. He may need special alterations to be sure his opportunities to learn are maximized.

These are examples of situational problems that will require special, tactical solutions. Some problems necessitate generating solutions for the whole group, some for small groups, and still others for individual children.

The very nature of tactical teaching is that it is planned in response to situational problems, so providing a list of tactical solutions for every problem is impossible. New teachers will develop their own repertoire of effective tactics as they gain experience. While the discussion in this chapter is focused on teaching, the same decision-making processes will be at play in dealing with situational problems of all types that inevitably arise in any classroom. The following are suggested starting places for developing tactical solutions to instructional problems. Describing the tactics separately is necessary to making them comprehensible, but in practice, there will be constant overlap among these tactics and between these tactics and the strategies described throughout this chapter. How this overlap plays out in the classroom is demonstrated in the examples given later in this chapter and in the comprehensive example of a week's teaching in Chapter 5.

Grouping

Grouping kindergartners into different sets at different times for different purposes ought to be standard procedure. In the ebb and flow of classroom activity, neither teachers nor children should be surprised when different groups are formed for different activities. Adjusting group size, deciding who will be included in what groups, and developing instructional experiences for particular groups are all elements of tactical problem solving. Group size can run from pairing children with one of their peers to forming a group of the whole that includes the entire class in a special activity. Numbers should be decided based on the needs and learning styles of the students, what teachers hope to accomplish, and the nature of the activities planned. The smaller the group, the more direct attention each child will be able to receive from the teacher. If the tasks to be completed are new or complex or the children in the group are those who usually need more support, then small groups will likely work better than large.

Who ends up in what groups will depend on the types of groups that are formed. As a general rule, children should have opportunities to work with all of their peers at some time or another and not be placed in the same group for every activity. While the teacher is usually in the position of making grouping decisions, when it's appropriate, children should be given opportunities to select in and out of their own groups. Groups that have utility in kindergarten include homogeneous ability groups, heterogeneous ability groups, interest or research groups, skills groups, and cooperative learning groups. I know of some school systems that require kindergarten teachers to form three reading groups based on achievement or ability, and to spend time with each group every day. Required or not, daily or not, there are times when grouping children homogeneously by ability is sound educational practice. There are also good reasons to use information about achievement or ability to purposefully form groups so that children at different levels have opportunities to work together (see the discussion of cooperative learning groups below). Interest or research groups are formed to give children the opportunity to work with others and go more deeply into a topic they care about. Teachers facilitate the formation of these groups and provide resources and instructional activities that meet the needs and interests of the groups. Skills groups are those formed by the teacher in order to teach certain children certain content that they need to master. These groups are ad hoc in the sense that they are formed in response to specific needs of specific children. In other words, they are not permanent groups that include the same children who get all their skills instruction in a group setting.

Cooperative learning groups are formed so that sets of children can work together to achieve a common end. There is a well-developed literature on cooperative learning as a vehicle for teaching content at the same time children are developing interpersonal skills outside the competitive goal structure that defines many classrooms (Johnson & Johnson, 1999; Slavin, 1995). While not all cooperative learning strategies are appropriate for young children, opportunities for applying cooperative grouping principles are available in kindergarten. Some important cooperative learning principles are that children with different backgrounds, different kinds of intelligence, and different abilities can work together to accomplish a common end; children can learn to take on different roles in order to facilitate group success; and children can improve their abilities to reflect on the learning process while processing information in concert with others. Cooperative grouping in kindergarten means setting up activities from which group products will be generated, assigning groups heterogeneously so that children with different perspectives will share in accomplishing a common end, and teaching children interpersonal skills such as listening, leading, following, being responsible, and supporting others. None of this happens without planning and careful monitoring, but cooperative groups can help teach important content and enhance children's interpersonal development.

Modeling and demonstrating

Modeling and demonstrating are often taken for granted in discussions of instruction. Everyone seems to understand that demonstrations and models are important teaching elements, but they are usually not discussed as overt, tactical approaches. One of the positive outcomes of the whole language movement is that teachers' modeling of real reading and writing processes is more widely acknowledged as a valuable tool for teaching literacy. The logic makes sense: Children want to be like those they admire and care about; when they see such individuals reading and writing, they want to imitate what those individuals are doing; by carefully modeling the actual processes of reading and writing, teachers make it possible for children to internalize those processes. Of course, this logic holds for content other than reading and writing. Children watch the activities of those they admire very closely and do their best to emulate what they see. By tactically modeling desirable learning behaviors for children, we enhance their chances for success.

Modeling and demonstrating are powerful tools for teaching a wide variety of curriculum elements.

Modeling is done without a running commentary about what's going on; teachers just openly and deliberately do what needs to be done (e.g., write a letter, sound out a word, or solve an addition problem). Adding commentary can be beneficial to coaching, discussed below, but modeling is just overtly doing what the teacher ultimately expects the child to do.

Demonstration is similar in that the teacher shows how something is done, but demonstrations involve more explanation and are usually associated with teaching substance more than process. When teaching children about the scientific properties of matter, for example, teachers demonstrate that water can take the form of a solid, liquid, or gas by showing how ice can be melted to a liquid state, then heated until it turns to steam. Reading or telling kindergartners about these changes will have far less impact than demonstrating. So, when teachers face situations involving whole classes, small groups, or individuals who need to learn skills, processes, or concepts, modeling and/or demonstrating can be effective tactics.

Coaching

Coaching usually involves modeling and demonstrating, but it goes beyond that to helping children practice what it is you want them to accomplish and giving them immediate feedback and more modeling/demonstration during the practice. Coaching is about moving students toward expert performance. Handwriting instruction, especially for those having difficulties on their own, is an example of an area in which coaching might be a good teaching tactic. The teacher may sit down with one or two students and show them how s/he makes an uppercase letter A. S/he talks about each stroke as s/he makes it, then asks the student to try it. As the student makes the lines, the teacher provides support at whatever level the child needs it. The teacher may place his/her hand over that of the child as the strokes are made, prompt the child verbally at each step, or repeat an earlier demonstration. Good coaching lets children know where they stand and provides the instruction and support necessary to help them be successful. Because coaching has a dynamic, interactive dimension between expert and learner, it cannot be done effectively with large groups. But for certain content, especially skills, it can be a powerful kindergarten teaching tactic.

Coaching can also be an effective tool for helping children develop cognitive strategies for monitoring and managing their own learning. As mentioned in Chapter 1, young children have the capacity to learn metacognitive tools for thinking about their own thinking (Bransford, Brown, & Cocking, 1999). With support from teachers, children can acquire cognitive strategies that help them understand and regulate how they remember, how they solve problems, and how they comprehend text (see Stanulis & Manning, 2003). Children do not stumble on these strategies accidentally; they learn them from teachers who are adept at coaching. The general approach is for teachers to think out loud with children, modeling an example of the thinking processes they want children to internalize. Children then say out loud what they are thinking as they attempt tasks, and teachers give feedback, hints, explanations, and more modeling. If memory strategies are the target area, kindergarten teachers may demonstrate how they remember facts by using verbal rehearsal (repeating the facts aloud) or rhythmic activities (reciting the facts as a poem or rap). If problem solving is the goal, teachers may verbalize the steps of a variety of ways to solve problems involving the kindergarten curriculum (e.g., creating an art project, solving a math problem, completing a puzzle, or reading an unknown word). If comprehension is the focus, kindergarten teachers model such strategies as generating questions (e.g., What are the characters trying to do?), summarizing (e.g., No one was happy in the end), and predicting what will happen next (e.g., I think she will run away because she is afraid) (Rosenshine & Meister, 1994).

Coaching as an instructional tactic can be applied at many levels in the kindergarten day. It is powerful for teaching basic content and for helping children develop sophisticated cognitive strategies. While it will take extra time to plan and implement coaching events, the benefits for students make it well worth the effort.

Tutoring

Tutoring is one-on-one teaching between a student and an adult or another child. The tutor works with the student on specific content with a specific teaching plan. Volunteers can (and should) have nonteaching interactions with children, but they are not tutoring during those contacts. All of the tactics described in this section could be used by the teacher in one-on-one settings, but I am interested here in making evident the possibilities of using other adults and older children as tutors. Other adults can be teaching assistants, parent or community volunteers, preservice teachers from local colleges doing placements in classrooms, or any other adult who is in a position to participate in tutoring a child. For kindergarten, I recommend that children who act as tutors be limited to those from upper grades, rather than from within the classroom. Many opportunities for children to interact one-on-one with other children in their classroom should be made available, but child-child tutoring sessions should be reserved for kindergartners matched with older children.

Tutoring can be an effective tactic for children who need one-on-one attention. The positive effects are increased when tutors have a clear idea of what they are supposed to do and are trained in how to do it. Adults may know the content to be taught without knowing what steps are required to teach it. Some student tutors may be unsure of the content and need clarification or review. Building in time to plan carefully what tutors are to do with whom and to prepare tutors for the tasks you want them to undertake will increase their effectiveness. Setting up a regular tutoring program with a local organization or an upper-grade classroom can be a great idea, and using assistants and individual volunteers can help students a lot; but maximizing the potential benefits of tutoring requires planning and preparation.

Discussing

Discussing can be a way to enrich children's understandings, apply newly learned content, and help students see connections between what they are learning and their own lives. Discussions are conversations between the teacher and groups of children around a particular topic. Some discussions take place with the whole class, others with groups as small as two or three. Discussions can take many forms appropriate for kindergarten. In some, teachers direct all the action and ask all the questions. In others, students take a more active role in directing the flow of conversation. Like all the teaching tactics described here, teachers will make decisions about how and when to use discussions based on instructional objectives and the needs of their students.

Guided discussions are a staple in elementary classrooms, especially during reading groups. In guided discussions, teachers take the most directive role. Teachers ask questions about content just covered, and responses are usually short answers that reveal children's understanding. The teacher can then either reinforce the responses or clarify misunderstandings. Lemlech (2002, p. 101) rightly notes that during guided discussions, "*co-action* rather than interaction occurs between teacher and student" (emphasis in original). Guided discussions have a place in kindergarten. Although kindergartners should have multiple opportunities for the give and take of genuine interaction, they need to learn the format and intent of guided discussions so that they can improve their abilities to concentrate on the essentials of a lesson.

At the other end of the spectrum are open-ended discussions that are used primarily to orient students to new content or help them see meaningful connections between their experiences and what they are learning. They are open-ended because there are no right or wrong answers and children offer ideas that go beyond reciting responses to teachers' direct questions. That does not mean that these discussions are without focus or purpose. Young children frequently have trouble staying on the topic of conversation, and teachers should be directive to the extent that they encourage children to keep their comments to the subject at hand. Open-ended discussions are most useful when new content in science, social studies, or health is introduced. For example, at the beginning of a study of roles and responsibilities, children may be asked to discuss what their jobs are at home and how they feel about doing them. This gets them oriented to the topic and sets up connections between their real-life experiences and the social studies content to be taught.

Semistructured discussions fall somewhere between the guided and open-ended varieties. Teachers provide more structure than in open-ended discussions but give the children more opportunities for interaction than in guided discussions. In most semistructured discussion settings, teachers and students understand that some product will be generated as a result of their discussion. Together, they may be producing a list, web, *K-W-L* chart, or some other

Discussions are useful for addressing all kinds of instructional issues.

graphic representation of what they are talking about. The list may be all their ideas for ways to find out about the weather. The web may show the links between the concepts they want to learn about related to animal habitats. The *K-W-L* chart may be a list of what they know (*K*) about personal health habits, followed by a list of what they want to learn (*W*) in that area. Another semistructured discussion of what they learned (*L*) could happen at the end of the study. The point is that children and teachers work together through the processes of discussion to produce something in concert. Teachers facilitate semistructured discussions and record responses; children offer suggestions and support each other's ideas.

Questioning is an important facet of discussions of all types. The kinds of questions teachers ask tell children what kind of thinking and participating they are expected to do. During guided discussions, most questions are designed to provoke memory skills by asking for factual information (e.g., In the story, who climbed over the wall first?). Participation means giving the teacher a short response and waiting to find out whether it is correct. Semistructured discussions give children a chance to reflect on their own understandings and apply them to the situation at hand. Questions signal children that individual thinking is valued and that multiple answers are desirable (e.g., What are all the ways we can think of to learn about working in a grocery store?). Open-ended discussions provide opportunities to encourage higher-level thinking. Even young children can be asked to apply information (e.g., What will happen if we repeat the experiment with more black and less white?), analyze situations (e.g., What happened in the story to make you think Mary was unhappy?), synthesize ideas (e.g., What could we put in our class book to tell others about the life cycle of a

APPLICATIONS

The kinds of questions teachers ask tell children what kind of thinking and participating they are expected to do.

Imagine that you are implementing a science unit on the human body, emphasizing that different body parts perform different functions. Using "functions of the skin" as your content, develop lists of questions for three kinds of discussions: guided, semistructured, and open-ended. Study your questions and anticipate the kinds of thinking children are likely to use and the kinds of participation you are likely to generate from each set of questions.

frog?), and evaluate options (e.g., Now that we know about healthy foods, which of these would you choose for a snack?).

Discussions are useful tools for addressing all kinds of instructional issues. It is important for kindergarten teachers to be aware of the potential of discussions for accomplishing different teaching purposes. Questions are ubiquitous in virtually all classrooms, but they can be used to better advantage when teachers see how they influence student thinking and define student participation. Different kinds of questions used in different kinds of discussions can be useful instructional tactics for kindergarten teachers.

Practicing

Practicing is an important part of the learning process that sometimes gets short shrift in discussions of early childhood teaching. We tend to lump drill and practice together and talk about them as if they were deadly sins. Although we understand that practice is essential for developing musical or athletic talent, we are reluctant to ask children to practice newly acquire skills in academic areas. I'm not advocating what have come to be known as drill-and-kill methods, where making children complete stacks of worksheets is taken to be the essence of teaching, but providing kindergartners the right kinds of practice can improve their learning.

Like questioning, the kind of practice you provide tells children a great deal about what is important and what you expect them to learn. For example, when kindergartners are learning to match written numerals to sets of objects, if the practice provided is a steady string of worksheets with pictures of objects and three numerals from which to select, children see that filling in bubbles or circling correct answers is what's important and completing their work is what they are supposed to do. But if practice means participating in a variety of activities that require them to match numerals with sets (e.g., matching dominos with numeral cards, playing a concentration game with peers, or doing a sorting activity with sets of plastic animals and numeral cards in the math center), children learn that the skill can be applied in many settings and that it is useful in a variety of meaningful ways. Practice for its own sake or as a way to occupy children's time is not what we're talking about here. Practice that helps children consolidate new knowledge and learn to apply new skills is our goal.

Practice can only happen after children have learned something new. Too many teachers try to use practice as a tool for teaching new content. They begin in the middle, assuming that the materials designed for practice will somehow teach children what they need to know. This phenomenon happens with both worksheet-driven practice and hands-on approaches. Instruction must happen before practice in order for the practice to have any utility. Giving children worksheets on digraphs or sending them to a center to play a digraph bingo game cannot teach them about digraphs or how to use them. In the same way, children who have had instruction but have not yet grasped the content should not be asked to practice what other students may be ready to do. This mistake leads children to experience frustration and failure and/or makes them practice doing things incorrectly.

Good practice activities provide children with feedback on how they are doing. This means that teachers must monitor children's practice and provide them with immediate information that tells them they are on the right track. If they are not, children need to be redirected so that their practice serves its intended ends. Good practice activities for kindergartners follow soon after instruction and are relatively short in duration. Waiting too long or asking too much will reduce the effectiveness of practice.

As mentioned above, good practice is varied and meaningful. Designing practice activities provides teachers with the chance to address differences in their students' learning styles and to apply principles related to multiple intelligences (see Chapter 1). Varying practice to include experiences with music, art, computers, nature, interpersonal interactions, and physical activity will go a long way toward helping each child connect with the content being learned.

Individualizing

Individualizing instruction means tailoring learning experiences to meet the needs of individual children. As a general concept, individualizing instruction is related to all the tactics described above. However, systematic approaches to individualization based on the concept of mastery learning have been developed, and knowing about them will give teachers more tactics to choose from as they react to children's instructional needs. **Mastery learning** was refined by Bloom and his colleagues (Block, 1971; Bloom, 1976; Carroll, 1971) in the 1970s, and it continues to influence teaching and learning today. The basic idea behind mastery learning is that what needs to be learned can be organized into a hierarchical sequence of learning objectives, and students should not move from one objective to the next without demonstrating mastery of the preceding objectives. Applying mastery learning principles usually means a sequence of pretesting, teaching, posttesting, and reteaching.

Individualization happens because mastery learning models are usually self-paced; that is, students work through materials designed to develop their mastery at whatever speed they are able. If they pass the pretest, they skip to the next objective. If they cannot demonstrate mastery on posttests after instruction, their progress is slowed because they need more instruction until they master that piece of content.

For kindergartners who are having difficulty in a particular area, the general model suggested by mastery learning may provide useful guidance. For example, children who do not seem to be moving forward in their literacy development may benefit from a careful analysis of what they can and cannot do in relation to the curriculum elements described in Chapter 2. Then systematic instruction can be planned and delivered to help them master elements that are causing difficulty. *Individualized* does not necessarily mean personalized. It may be that more than one child needs systematic instruction at the same time. While I would not recommend mastery learning approaches as the centerpiece of kindergarten instructional practice, I do recommend that teachers view it as a viable tactic for addressing particular classroom issues. I see all of the tactics described in this section as possible alternatives for maximizing the learning of kindergarten children, and I believe using (or even considering) a wide variety of alternatives will help teachers develop their own stockpiles of modifications and elaborations.

Effective practice activities provide children with direct feedback on how they are doing.

Direct teaching

Like mastery learning, **direct teaching** has its theoretical roots in behaviorism. It is on the opposite end of the teaching strategies continuum because it is so different from incidental teaching. Rather than creating teachable moments by designing activities that ask students to operate just beyond their level of independent functioning, direct teaching means that teachers organize content in a logical sequence and systematically teach that content in a direct way. Direct teaching is based on the assumption that knowledge exists outside the learner, and it's the teacher's job to transfer that knowledge to students. Teachers know what needs to be learned, and they are responsible for directing that learning as efficiently as possible.

Direct teaching in early childhood education is usually associated with approaches such as DISTAR or the Bereiter-Engelmann model, which were widely used in Head Start and Follow Through programs as part of efforts to teach "disadvantaged" children during the 1970s and 1980s (Goffin & Wilson, 2001). This type of direct teaching depended on scripted lessons that were carried out "in a business-like, task-oriented manner" (Bereiter & Engelmann, 1966, p. 59). Lessons were done with small groups, were fast-paced, and required frequent verbal responses to which immediate feedback was given. Carnine, Carnine, Karp, and Weisberg (1988) provide a brief description of the elements of direct instruction for kindergarten:

> The group activities are composed of short segments that focus on specific skills or a combination of previously taught skills. Teachers explain, demonstrate, and ask questions for 15 to 20 minutes in each subject area. . . . The lessons, which include frequent teacher-pupil verbal interaction through many games and races, provide children with a great deal of active participation in the lessons and high engagement rates of as many as 10 responses per minute. (p. 74)

In classrooms beyond preschools and kindergartens, several forms of direct teaching were developed. Many of these were based on process-product studies that looked at what exact teaching behaviors (processes) were associated with improved academic performance as measured on standardized test scores (products). Slavin (1997) identified a set of effective lesson components synthesized from the work of a number of advocates of direct instruction approaches. To establish a framework for doing direct teaching in the new kindergarten, I have adapted Slavin's components to include the following steps:

1. Set the stage for learning.
2. Present new material.
3. Monitor and adjust.
4. Provide independent practice.

What follows is a description of how each step might look in the new kindergarten. After these steps are described, strengths and weaknesses of direct teaching are discussed and ways to utilize this strategy effectively suggested.

1.   Set the stage for learning

When teachers **set the stage for learning,** they orient their students to what is to follow in the lesson. The idea is to signal students that a new lesson is beginning, to capture their attention, and to give them a reason to become engaged. Setting the stage can have several components, and which components the teacher selects for a particular lesson depends on the kind of lesson involved. One essential component is providing a context for the new learning. This means helping children see connections between new material and what they have already learned in school or what they experience in their everyday lives. Another component is naming the learning. Direct teaching is objective-driven. Specific instructional objectives are identified for each lesson, and the process-product research indicates that telling children the objective (what they will be able to do at the end of the lesson) improves performance (Rosenshine & Stevens, 1986). Another component is grabbing their attention. High-interest props, an engaging picture book, or a catchy rhyme can serve as a "grabber" to orient students to the lesson and make them want to participate.

2.   Present new material

The second step in the direct teaching model is to **present new material.** At this stage the teacher actually "teaches" the content of the lesson. The form of that teaching is didactic. Teachers tell the students what they want them to know, demonstrate how that knowledge is applied, and model what the children are supposed to be able to do at the end of the lesson. The intent is not for children to discover the learning through activity or discussion; teachers tell children what they need to know, then show them how it works. If the content is a concept, teachers define the concept and give several examples. If a skill needs to be learned, teachers describe the skill and demonstrate several examples of how to do it. When it's efficiently done, all this teaching is tied to the instructional objective for the lesson. Teachers are telling and showing students how to do what they will be expected to do at the end of the lesson.

3. Monitor and adjust

Monitor and adjust is what teachers do after they present new material to find out whether their students have learned that material. Children are given the chance to apply the new learning immediately and in the presence of the teacher, so that teacher feedback can be given on the spot. Again, students should be asked to do what they have just observed the teacher doing. In small groups, the teacher can go from student to student, asking the child to perform the required task. In a large group, other devices such as individual dry-erase boards or thumbs-up signs can be used to monitor children's learning. The idea is to monitor what they have learned by giving children chances to demonstrate their learning immediately after the teaching and to adjust instruction, or reteach, when it becomes apparent that all or some children do not understand.

4. Provide independent practice

Teachers complete the direct teaching cycle when they **provide independent practice**. The teacher helps children consolidate their new understanding by giving them a chance to use it right away. In kindergarten, involved homework assignments or pages of worksheets are not effective as independent practice. Still, once new learning is introduced, kindergartners need opportunities to practice using their new knowledge. Simple homework assignments that are arranged so that parents can help (e.g., Bring in a set of six objects) or short seatwork activities (e.g., Circle the pictures that start with t) are good independent practice options, as are center activities and games. The logic is simple: Give children a chance to practice doing what they have just learned to do so that they will not forget how to do it.

APPLICATIONS

Monitor and adjust is what teachers do after they present new material to find out whether their students have learned that material.

Imagine that you are using direct teaching with a small group of children who are having difficulty with the concept of one-to-one correspondence. Develop a monitor-and-adjust activity that you would use immediately after you presented new material on and examples of how to do one-to-one correspondence. Along with producing any materials you will need, write out a set of steps you will follow to determine whether students get it (monitor) and what you will do for those children who need more help (adjust).

Direct teaching is an important instructional strategy. It is not appropriate for every kind of learning in kindergarten, but it is a powerful tool for helping all children learn certain kinds of content and for helping some children learn content that they are not getting any other way. The major strengths of direct teaching are its clarity and efficiency. The direct part of direct instruction leaves little doubt in the minds of the teacher or students about what is being done and how it fits in the overall picture. Objectives are clear, teaching and practice are clearly tied to objectives, and outcomes are either met or they are not. The model is efficient. Teachers know what is to be taught, they design lessons that get at important content directly, and they keep children focused on lesson objectives throughout. Two weaknesses of direct teaching are that it reduces child input and that it does not work well for teaching children how to think. In order for lessons to be efficient, they must be teacher directed, meaning that children's spontaneous responses will be discouraged. In this model, correct responses are what count and the thinking behind the responses is of little concern. As a consequence, overuse of direct teaching reduces children's chances of understanding and improving their own thinking processes.

Direct teaching works best when the content consists of basic skills and concepts. If the learning can be expressed as a behavioral objective (e.g., the learner will match upper- and lowercase letters), then direct teaching may be a good option. If the object is to help children learn to do complex tasks (e.g., solving problems), incidental, thematic, or tactical approaches may be better. In addition, certain children may learn best when direct teaching strategies are used. In some classrooms, there may be several students for whom direct teaching is the most effective strategy. Part of the job of the new kindergarten teacher is to figure out what strategies will work with which students so that all children have the opportunity to maximize their potential.

Using the Continuum—Examples of Incidental, Thematic, Strategic, and Direct Teaching

In order to give teachers a sense of what it might look like to apply the continuum of teaching strategies in a kindergarten, this section presents a series of specific examples showing how content from the curriculum presented in Chapter 2 can be taught in a variety of ways. An example of using incidental, thematic, tactical, and direct teaching in each of the subject matter areas of the curriculum is presented. Examples are necessarily brief and disconnected—they are just meant to help readers see the possibilities of applying strategies across the teaching continuum to content across the curriculum. In Chapter 5, a detailed description of an entire week's instruction is presented, showing how the continuum can be applied over time and fit together into a meaningful whole.

Language Arts

Incidental

Simple text reading provides an ideal opportunity for incidental teaching. Teachers join with individual (or small groups of) children, sharing text that the child can read with assistance. The teacher supplies scaffolding when the child needs it. The scaffolding that the teacher provides teaches children the ways that competent readers operate on text.

Thematic

Correspondence between spoken and written words can be built into activities that are part of integrated theme studies. Asking children to help make a chart that summarizes what they have learned at the end of a week-long study of spiders gives them the opportunity to summarize what they have learned and to see that what they have to say can be written down as they say it and read back immediately and later.

Tactical

Writing upper- and lowercase letters is content that some children might learn best with the help of a tutor. Training an adult to work with a particular child on particular letters using specific methods can be a major benefit to children's handwriting development. The methods should include the expectation that the tutor will demonstrate correct letter formation and support children's efforts to duplicate that demonstration. When the child already knows how to write the letters, tutoring is not needed.

Direct

Letter-sound correspondence can be taught using direct instruction methods. The letter *m* and the /m/ sound could be introduced in a teacher-directed lesson that includes setting the stage (reviewing the letters and letter sounds they've been working with, reading an alliterative poem with lots of initial /m/ sounds, and telling the children they will be learning that *m* makes the /m/ sound); presenting new material (telling children that *m* makes the sound that starts *monkey*, demonstrating how to make the /m/ sound, and giving lots

Alliterative poems and songs are good vehicles for helping children learn letter-sound correspondence.

of examples of objects that start with *m*); monitoring and adjusting (giving children opportunities to demonstrate the /*m*/ sound, to recite the rule that *m* spells the sound that starts *monkey*, and to identify objects that start with *m*, while the teacher gives feedback on their attempts and reteaches where necessary); and providing independent practice (setting up a learning center activity where children sort objects by the beginning sounds that have been introduced).

Mathematics

Incidental

Numerals are content that can be emphasized at teachable moments throughout the day. Whenever opportunities for counting present themselves, incidental teaching of numerals ought to be included. When kindergartners are counting the number of children who are absent, the number of sunny days so far this month, the number of spots available in the art center, or the number of children who have turned six, teachers should write the numerals that represent those numbers and explain that the numerals are a record of the number of items just counted. This teaches children to associate numerals with numbers and that the numerals represent a constant number of items.

Thematic

Nonstandard measurement can be taught as part of a project study of a topic such as shadows. The length of shadows can be calculated at different times of day by cutting string to represent the lengths of shadows cast by different objects or by lining up unsharpened pencils to see how many equal the lengths of the shadows. Making graphs to represent this information, then analyzing the relationships between time of day and length of shadows, teaches other important math (and science) concepts.

Tactical

Comparing and ordering is content that can be taught using cooperative grouping strategies. Children could be assigned to heterogeneous groups and each group asked to order sets of objects based on a variety of attributes. For example, rods of various lengths could be ordered from longest to shortest, balls ordered from smallest to largest, or plastic animals ordered from tallest to shortest. The tactic is to get children with well-developed comparison skills to help other children develop those skills in cooperative groups.

Direct

Ordinal numbers can be introduced in a large-group, direct teaching lesson. Setting the stage might include reminding children how they determine who comes in first, second, or third in a race, reviewing simple counting from 1 through 5, and telling children that they will learn a new way to count from first through fifth. Presenting new material could include telling children that ordinal counting is one way we order objects; demonstrating how to count objects from first through fifth; and explaining how ordinal counting can be used to tell what comes first, second, third, fourth, or fifth. Monitoring and adjusting could involve asking children to count using ordinals and to determine the ordinal position of objects in linear sets of five. Independent practice could be a board game that requires children to determine the order of finish for five race cars.

Science

Incidental

Observation is a science process that can be improved through incidental teaching. Learning how to observe carefully means using our senses to their full capacity. It means paying attention to details and concentrating on specific attributes. When children are given opportunities to use their senses in science activities such as examining the properties of matter, teachers can scaffold children's observation attempts by asking guiding questions, pointing out subtleties, and suggesting strategies for improving observational accuracy.

Thematic

Plants provide a good basis for integrated theme studies. In fact, science content in general provides great topics for units, projects, or integrated theme studies. An example of an integrated theme study activity would be to help students plan a plant experiment in which they compare the results of giving some plants soil, water, and sunlight, some soil and water only, and some soil and sunlight only. Students hypothesize about what they think will happen, keep a careful record of results day to day, and form conclusions and interpretations at the end of the experiment.

Tactical

Weather provides content that can be organized into tactical teaching activities. Forming an interest group of children who are fascinated by lightning is an example of one tactic. The group can be given the task of teaching the rest of the class what lightning is and how it works. Access to resources such as books, Internet sites, and educational videos will need to be provided, as will support in how to use the resources and report the findings. Librarians and media personnel can help with the resources, and older students, classroom assistants, and/or volunteers can help with the support.

Direct

The body provides content that can be taught directly. A lesson introducing the sense of smell might include setting the stage by having children close their eyes and guess what you are holding as you move among them with an open bottle of pickle juice, then telling them they are going to learn how they can use their sense of smell to take in information about the world. Presenting new material could include telling children that their noses are valuable tools for making observations and giving examples of situations when their sense of smell can tell them things that their other senses cannot (e.g., smelling smoke or figuring out what is cooking in the other room). Monitor and adjust could involve having children guess substances, by smell, that you have collected in opaque jars, and independent practice might be having children place a smiley face on a graph you have designed to record each child's favorite smell from your collection.

Social Studies

Incidental

Shared and unique characteristics of self can be reinforced at many times during the school day. The outcomes we want are for children to understand that they are special individuals because they have qualities that make them unique and that they are part of a community because they have qualities that make them the same as others. Some children may need support to understand that they are special individuals; others may need help seeing that they are part of a community. Incidental teaching will involve finding situations in which teachers can scaffold children's learning in either direction. These situations might occur when children are working in centers, in small groups, or one-on-one with the teacher.

Thematic

Growth and change can be the topic of a unit of instruction. Focusing a series of lessons on how kindergartners' bodies have grown and changed in their short lives is a good example. Children could be encouraged to bring in pictures of babies, toddlers, preschoolers, and kindergartners. These could form the basis for lessons describing how humans grow and change over a lifetime.

Tactical

Rules and laws can be taught as part of semistructured discussions. Many teachers like to involve their students in the generation of classroom rules. It is possible to set up a semistructured discussion that has as its purpose the creation of rules for classroom behavior (or lunchroom, recess, or field-trip behavior). This kind of work may be difficult for some kindergartners and should not become a brainstorming session in which any suggestion is accepted. It should be a genuine discussion in which the teacher takes the lead in guiding the children to construct reasonable rules.

Direct

Production, distribution, and consumption are basic economic concepts that can be introduced directly. A direct teaching lesson on how milk gets from the cow to the lunchroom is one example. The teacher may set the stage by reading a nonfiction picture book about dairy farming, then explaining that today students are going to learn where the milk they drink at lunch came from. New information could be presented by going back to the picture book and highlighting the steps: milking the cows, pasteurizing and packaging the milk, loading the milk onto trucks, and delivering the milk to its destination. Monitor and adjust could involve having children retell the story and/or describe the steps in the process. Independent practice might be drawing a picture that shows how milk is produced, distributed, and consumed.

Health and physical education

Incidental

Body awareness can be taught incidentally in the spaces of the classroom, playground, and gymnasium. Helping children become more aware of their bodies and how they move in relation to the space around them is a constant challenge in kindergarten. Many incidental opportunities are created throughout the day when children can be reminded of the limits of their personal space and of their responsibilities to manage themselves within that space. I am talking about teaching here, not scolding or berating young children. Children need to learn body awareness, and scaffolding their attempts do so is part of teaching kindergarten.

Thematic

Nutrition involves content that can easily be adapted to thematic teaching. It's easy to imagine an integrated theme study of healthy snacks, for example. A culminating activity for such a study might be planning, preparing, cooking, and eating a variety of healthy snacks. Parents, neighboring classrooms, or other guests could be invited to share in the treats and find out what the children have learned during their thematic study.

Tactical

Movement may be best taught using coaching methods. Athletes, dancers, and others for whom movement is essential are used to learning or refining movements with the help of a coach. Both fine- and large-motor skills can be enhanced when teachers use a coaching cycle that includes modeling, demonstrating, assisted practice, feedback, and more modeling and demonstrating. Some schools have physical education teachers who teach movement as a part of their curricula, but coaching movement development is also the job of the kindergarten teacher.

Direct

Safety rules and their importance can be taught directly. A direct teaching lesson on procedures for reporting emergencies is an example. Setting the stage might include reviewing the importance of staying safe and getting help when dangerous situations arise, asking children what kinds of situations might require the help of others, and telling them that today they are going to learn how to report emergencies using the phone. New information would be describing and demonstrating when and how to call 911. Monitoring and adjusting would be giving each child the opportunity to role-play dialing 911 and telling the operator about an imaginary danger. Independent practice might include setting up a pretend emergency phone in the housekeeping center and encouraging its use during children's socio-dramatic play.

Art and music

Incidental

Deriving meaning from art can be taught whenever direct experiences with art present themselves in the classroom. A good example is taking advantage of the art found in high-quality picture books. Helping children see the importance of art as a medium for communicating ideas and feelings should be a natural part of sharing books. Children can learn to see illustrators as artists who make significant contributions to the enjoyment of reading, and more generally, they can learn to understand the power of art to evoke thoughts and emotions.

Thematic

Deriving meaning from music is an aesthetic goal that could be addressed through thematic teaching. Singing and movement should be part of almost all thematic teaching strategies, and opportunities to be exposed to musical genres and artists should be included as well. For example, an integrated theme study of bees or insects might include listening to, discussing, and moving in response to the "Flight of the Bumblebee" by Rimsky-Korsakov.

Tactical

Creating art may be taught by modeling and demonstration. As mentioned in Chapter 1, the Reggio Emilia preschools in Italy have taught us that children's capacities for creating art can be enhanced significantly with the guidance of adults. In the Reggio schools, *atelieristas* (artists in residence) are a critical part of the teaching staffs who work directly with children to model and demonstrate how art is made. Although fewer and fewer schools provide art instruction and few kindergarten teachers see themselves as artists, opportunities to model and demonstrate techniques for creating art in a variety of media should be taken advantage of.

Direct

Elements of art such as color, line, texture, shape, and space can be taught using direct teaching approaches. We usually don't associate direct teaching with art, but it is possible to teach art concepts (e.g., shape) using structured lessons. Setting the stage for a lesson on shape might include reviewing the geometric shapes, telling children that all art is made up of shapes, and explaining that today they are going to learn to find shapes in works of art. New information would be showing the students art reproductions and pointing out the geometric shapes found within them. Monitor and adjust could be presenting new art objects and asking children to find the shapes. Independent practice could be having the children produce their own art using circles, squares, triangles, and rectangles.

Closing Thoughts

As the examples demonstrate, the strategies on the teaching continuum are not mutually exclusive. Incidental teaching, for example, can be used as part of tactical strategies such as coaching, and thematic strategies can include elements of independent practice that could fit the direct teaching mode. The continuum simply gives teachers a way to broaden their perspectives on what is possible and appropriate as they make instructional decisions. It's a framework for thinking about how best to teach kindergarten content in ways that recognize the individual differences and needs of children, and it's a tool for thinking of ways to maximize children's chances of meeting the academic standards of contemporary kindergarten classrooms. The teaching strategies continuum and this book are about teaching the child *and* meeting the standards.

Much of the field of early childhood education is divided into camps that promote either child-centered or academic approaches. Kindergarten teachers feel trapped when their training is based on child-centered assumptions and the expectations of their jobs are mostly academic. Dichotomizing the complexities of kindergarten teaching into either/or categories ignores the real world of public school teaching, distorts what is known about learning and development, and places new teachers under tremendous pressure. The central idea of this book is that it is possible to provide high quality kindergarten programs that acknowledge the real world of teaching in public school settings, synthesize current knowledge of learning and development, and help teachers make good decisions that meet children's needs and improve their chances for academic success.

In this chapter, I have argued that effective teachers are active decision makers. It's their job to know their children, their communities, and their parents.

It's their job to understand the expectations of the systems within which they work. It's their job to have a firm grasp of the curriculum that needs to be taught. It's their job to have a variety of teaching strategies available so that they can teach the curriculum effectively. And it's their job to bring it all together in a way that ensures every child is successful as a person and a student.

Good decisions come from balancing the complexities of teaching in the new kindergarten. Good decisions come from putting together curriculum and instruction in ways that engage kindergartners in real learning. And good decisions come from wise teachers who understand that they can teach the child and meet the standards.

FOR YOUR CONSIDERATION

1. What characteristics, qualities, and competencies do kindergarten teachers need in order to be professional problem solvers?

2. What are the advantages and disadvantages of using incidental teaching strategies in the kindergarten classroom?

3. What are similarities and differences among units, projects, and integrated theme studies?

4. What are the strengths and weaknesses of homogeneous and heterogeneous grouping tactics?

5. What is the place (if any) of direct instruction in kindergarten?

LEARNING ACTIVITIES

INDIVIDUAL ACTIVITIES

- Select a kindergartner and set up a one-on-one learning situation in which you apply incidental strategies to teach the child a mathematics skill or concept that is within his or her zone of proximal development. Make an audio or videotape of the teaching event and analyze the tape to see how close you came to the scaffolding elements described in this chapter.

Continues

LEARNING ACTIVITIES *continued*

- Examine materials such as teachers' editions of adopted textbook series, state and district handbooks, and commercial programs that kindergarten teachers are given to teach social studies (or any subject area). Using the continuum of teaching strategies in this chapter, analyze the materials to see which teaching strategies are encouraged, discouraged, or ignored.

SMALL GROUP ACTIVITIES

- Brainstorm all the activities you can think of to teach curriculum content in a particular subject area (e.g., Language Arts—Reading) within the context of an integrated thematic study of rain (or another science-related topic). Have a recorder write down your ideas, then go back to the list and note how much content from other areas of the curriculum is addressed in your group's activities.

- Plan and teach a short lesson to members of your group using direct teaching strategies. Pick language arts or mathematics content suitable for direct teaching, teach the lesson to your peers (who will role-play being kindergartners) while being videotaped, watch the video together, and offer constructive criticism on how well the elements of the direct teaching were addressed.

LARGE GROUP ACTIVITIES

- Organize the class into two teams and debate the relative merits of academic versus developmental kindergarten programs. Pretend that each team represents groups of teachers who want the district policy to be either fully academic or fully developmental. Teams prepare their arguments, present their cases, cross-examine their opponents, and then debrief on how they really feel about the issues raised.

- Help the class identify a problematic situation students have observed in their kindergarten experiences. Use the problem-solving model described in this chapter to take them through the processes of systematically analyzing a problem and generating viable alternatives. Have plenty of board space to record their ideas as you go through each step, and help them reflect on the process once complete.

CHAPTER | 4

How Do I Organize and Manage a New Kindergarten Classroom?

KEY TERMS AND CONCEPTS

Learning as purpose	Routines
Community of learners	Transitions
Classroom rules	Dynamic assessment
Classroom spatial arrangements	Documentation
Learning center	Inclusion
Learning versus fun	Individual education program
Classroom schedules	Reciprocal relationships
Special areas	Community mapping
Modified full-day kindergarten	Problem-solving model

One of the themes of this book is balance. Good teaching means finding and maintaining a balance across the spectrum of what makes kindergartens work. The previous two chapters were about balancing curriculum and instruction in ways that recognize the complex world in which kindergarten teachers work. This chapter applies the theme of balance to setting up and running effective classrooms. The trick is to resist the temptation of reducing the world to black/white, either/or alternatives. We are not looking for the midpoint between extreme positions. Rather, the balance we are after involves processing information from the particular circumstances of each classroom, understanding the dynamic factors that surround particular schools and communities, and implementing a variety of alternatives from a variety of perspectives.

Learning ought to be the purpose of kindergarten.

Classroom management is the major concern of most new teachers. We have all been socialized into thinking that there must be one best way to solve all problems, including how to manage kindergartners' behavior. The trouble is there is no single best way. Living in the postmodern world has taught us that those who claim to have "the answer" are usually ideologues or entrepreneurs who have found a way to profit from taking a narrow view of complex issues. It is wiser to expect and accept complexity and try to find answers that solve problems for now. Balancing the application of those answers is what organizing and managing the new kindergarten is all about.

This chapter focuses on elements of classroom organization and management that must be balanced in order to maximize opportunities to teach the child and meet the standards. Although elements such as space, time, activity, rights and responsibilities, assessment, ability levels, and parent/community involvement are treated in separate sections, they are united around the central notion of **learning as purpose.** I believe schooling has lost its sense of purpose. Students often don't know why they are in school, why they should work hard, or why they should behave. Without a purpose for being there, students see school as a place defined by meaningless activity and arbitrary control. Establishing a purpose gives teachers, students, parents, and administrators a shared perspective from which to build sound classroom organization and management.

On my desk, I keep a photograph of my last kindergarten class, a typical shot of the teacher and his students lined up in the classroom. I keep it in front of me to remind me why I am working in the field of early childhood education. Behind my students and me is a bulletin board that says in large cutout letters, "Learn a little every day." This was our class motto, and it expresses what I think the purpose of kindergarten (and all schooling) ought to be: learning.

One of my first goals was to teach my students what learning is. I am convinced that schools are so consumed with products and performance (e.g., worksheets, end-of-unit assessments, standardized test scores) that many children never figure out what learning is, let alone how to do it. I gave my students tasks slightly above their operating level—activities that I knew they knew they couldn't do alone. I guided them in whatever way was necessary to move them to the next level. As we worked together, I helped them step back and look at the process we were going through, and I celebrated with them the fact that they had learned.

Our motto drove everything we did, and the act of learning a little every day was taken as our mutual goal. We called ourselves the K Team. Everything about the classroom sent the message that learning is what counts and that we will learn together. That everyone could, should, and would learn became the defining ethic of our school lives. We were a community of learners before that phrase became popular.

A **community of learners** exists in any setting where learning is valued by everyone and where everyone is responsible for the learning of everyone else. Most schools are set up on a scarce resources model: There's only so much learning, so much achievement, so much attention, and so many good grades available. The students' job is to make sure they get their share. So the top students get all the good grades and almost all of the positive attention, achievement, and learning. The other students take what's left. In this scarce resources classroom economy, confidence that you are a capable learner is hard to come by. In a community of learners, the act of learning is spotlighted and valued as inherently good. There is no finite amount of learning, achievement, or attention to be used up by a few. There's an unlimited amount, and everyone's learning is celebrated. Learning is the purpose of school.

When a community of learners is established around a common purpose, everyone who has a part in the classroom has a reference point on which to base decisions. When teachers set up the physical arrangements of the classroom, make a class schedule, decide what should be taught—and when and how—and design assessment strategies, the core question they must answer is,

"How will this effect learning?" When children and teachers decide on classroom rules or when children decide among alternative behaviors in the classroom, the core question should be, "How will this effect learning?" When parents are invited to participate in classrooms or when conflicts arise between school and home, the essential question ought to be, "How will this effect learning?" And when the equilibrium of the classroom needs adjusting, as it always will, the key question is, "How will this effect learning?"

Purposeful activity is the glue that holds successful kindergarten programs together. Without the glue, the elements of any program will separate and lose their meaning. In terms of organization, lack of purpose means fragmentation and confusion. In terms of management, it means power struggles and alienation.

The rest of this chapter describes approaches to balancing elements of a successful kindergarten classroom. The balance within each element depends on the establishment of a shared purpose. Purposes other than learning are possible—socialization, enculturation, cultural transmission, democratization, self-fulfillment, achievement, basic skills mastery, preparation for work—but I will discuss finding a balance based on the assumption that learning ought to be the purpose of school. The general model would still hold, but it's clear that the balance would shift in dramatic ways if other purposes were adopted.

Balancing Rights and Responsibilities— Everyone Is Responsible for Accomplishing the Purposes of the Group

The K Team came to school every day expecting to learn. From my first contacts with parents and students before school started, I emphasized my conviction that each and every child was going to learn something important every day. As the year began, I spent time establishing that we were a learning team, that every member of the team was going to learn, and that we were all going to participate in the learning of everyone else. I put everyone's picture on the "K Team" bulletin board, and I put up and explained the "Learn a little every day" bulletin board. We talked about learning, I began the process of showing them what learning is, and I modeled for them the joy of knowing that learning is happening.

For me, this is no gimmick. It is not a way to manipulate kids. Establishing a purpose is the opposite of a canned program for managing children's behavior. Typical management strategies start from the outside and (good ones) attempt to work in. That is, they seek to give adults the ability to control children's behavior, then hope that children will internalize their own self-regulation. Some aspects of these management strategies are necessary and effective for solving classroom problems, but establishing a shared purpose makes possible a different classroom dynamic. When everyone buys into the notion that learning is what drives everything, then there is always a tangible reason to do the right thing or at least to avoid doing things that hurt the chances of others to learn. The teacher is part of the learning community, and he/she is ultimately responsible for everything that happens in the classroom, but everyone shares responsibility for everyone else's learning.

To help beginning kindergartners learn how to support the learning of everyone else, I established very simple **classroom rules.** I did not go through a process of guiding children to create classroom rules. Although I think this can be a valuable learning activity that teaches important social studies content, it can lead to long lists of specific rules and consequences that overwhelm some children and invite others to make legalistic interpretations ("It doesn't say I can't do that"). My approach to helping children create rules was to wait for a few months, then let them design rules for smaller parts of the classroom day (e.g., going to lunch, getting ready to go home). My intent at the start of the year was to build a classroom community around learning as a common purpose, and I wanted our general classroom rules to build logically from that purpose. The classroom rules for the K Team were:

1. We are the K Team, and we are here to learn.
2. We learn best when we feel safe and happy.
3. We will help each other learn a little every day.

The rules were prominently displayed above the K Team bulletin board, and we went over them several times at the beginning of the year. It's important to make the rules as clear as possible and to explain what they mean in terms of children's behavior (e.g., "When you are wandering around the room, are you learning?" Or "When you do something to make others feel afraid or sad, are you helping them learn?"). But the real power of these simple rules is in redirecting children's behavior. At this point the rules come to life for children. When one child is intimidating another either physically or verbally, the rules make it clear that someone else's chances to learn are jeopardized. A rule says that everyone must have every chance to learn is much different than a rule that says no hitting or no threatening. In the case of the latter, the teacher becomes the police officer and judge, and the child's reason for not hitting or threatening is to avoid getting caught.

APPLICATIONS

To help beginning kindergartners learn how to support the learning of every-one else, I established very simple classroom rules based on our shared commitment to being a learning team.

Imagine that your school is implementing a schoolwide behavior management system based on having children turn a succession of cards as their misbehavior escalates. The principal and the consultant hired to train teachers on using the system tell you that everyone must use the system so that classroom management is consistent across the school. Describe how you will meet the spirit of the schoolwide discipline plan, while continuing to use your classroom rules as the basis for teaching children to be responsible for themselves by being responsive to the learning needs of others.

When children have a purpose for being in school, accomplishing that purpose can be the motivation that undergirds everything that happens there. When children are mischievous, forgetful, or even angry, referring to simple rules like those I've suggested gives them a reason to change their behavior without turning classroom management into a power struggle or an exercise in behavior manipulation. By reminding children of the rules and consistently referring directly to those rules when disruptions occur, you teach children to monitor their own behavior and to help others safeguard the integrity of the learning community.

Establishing a shared purpose will not be easy in every setting; some children may never buy into learning as the reason for being in kindergarten, but I can tell you that I have used this approach successfully in schools where skeptics predicted it wouldn't have a chance and with children whom others had already written off. It helps a lot that I truly believe learning is what school ought to be about. When I taught kindergarten classes a few years ago and as I volunteer in classrooms today, my reason for being there is to help children learn. I think most kindergarten teachers are there for the same reason. A colleague of mine and I analyzed prospective teachers' reasons for selecting early childhood education as a career. Our findings indicate that new teachers are a lot like me. Two of their most frequently cited reasons for wanting to teach are because they love children and because they enjoy seeing them learn (Phillips & Hatch, 2000a).

But loving children isn't enough. Unless we are helping them learn, we are missing the opportunity to utilize our emotional commitment to improve their chances to have full, enriched lives.

Making learning the centerpiece of kindergarten programs is possible for almost all teachers. It takes effort, consistency, and commitment. It's hard work to establish learning as a class ethos; it's easy to slip and be inconsistent in tying children's behavior to the classroom rules; and it's impossible to "sell" learning as the purpose of school if you are not committed to the idea yourself. But the rewards of such an approach far outweigh the costs. When children (and adults) operate from a shared understanding of what is really important, dealing with the inevitable rough spots becomes much more manageable than trying to work within a system in which controlling children is the principal objective. From my perspective, an ethos of classroom control means nothing but rough spots. In any classroom, teachers are the adults in charge, and it's important to their sense of security that children know teachers are in charge. Still, balancing the responsibilities of everyone in the classroom can lead to the development of learning communities in which everyone's rights are secure. The remainder of this chapter is about other dimensions of classroom balance, but all depend on the central idea that learning is the shared purpose of schooling.

Balancing the Arrangement of Space— Every Space Has a Purpose

As new teachers contemplate their first jobs, among the decisions they face is their **classroom spatial arrangements.** This means taking inventory of the available furniture, materials, storage, and wall space. It also means looking at what other kindergarten teachers have done with their rooms and finding out what limits on your creativity might be imposed by building or district rules and regulations. Getting a broad idea of what's there and what's generally expected will provide necessary context for the many decisions associated with setting up a classroom.

In this section, I provide a set of questions and some alternatives to guide teachers' decision making about using the space in a new kindergarten classroom. Every context, every space, and every teacher will be different, so prepackaged formulas will not work. One principle that ought to guide all decisions about the arrangement of space is that every space should have a purpose.

And if learning is the purpose of school, every space ought to contribute to children's opportunities to learn.

Whose space is it?

The ways classrooms are set up speak volumes about what is valued there. I have seen classrooms that are beautifully decorated and always in order. The decorations usually come from the local school supply store, and the order usually means that there's a place for everything and everything is in its place. At the other extreme are classrooms that are simply chaotic. No apparent attention has been paid to the aesthetics of the display space, and order seems to be random, at best. Good teachers can be doing good work in both of these extreme conditions, but what do these kinds of classrooms say to children (and others) about what is supposed to happen there? Too much tidiness may communicate that the classroom belongs to the teacher and that what counts as beauty is commercially produced and what counts as organization is compulsive neatness. Absolute chaos may signal that the classroom belongs to no one (at least no one seems to care about its appearance) and that being organized is not important. Neither fits my criterion that space ought to reflect learning as the reason to have a classroom in the first place.

In a community devoted to learning, it makes sense that the classroom space belongs to everyone. It's not the exclusive space of the students or their teachers; it's the shared space in which learning happens. Display space will likely include teacher-planned materials, including commercially produced items, as well as student-produced materials, such as art work, group experience stories, and project constructions and documentation. That space and the rest of the classroom will have an order to it that children understand and have a hand in maintaining. It's not order for its own sake, but order so that learning can happen. The next subsections describe what that order might look like, but students' and teachers' answer to the "Whose space is it?" question has to be *ours*.

How will space be organized?

Several rules of thumb for arranging the kindergarten space need to be mentioned here. They are not prescriptions that must be followed, but guidelines that have been helpful to early childhood teachers over the years. Considering these guidelines will help teachers establish meaningful order and make better decisions about classroom organization.

- Supplies that children will use should be stored in such a way that children can be responsible for taking out and putting back what they need.

- Materials that are to be used another time or that are not for children's use should be stored separately from what is currently in use.

- Storage cabinets should double as partitions or room dividers whenever possible.

- Personal storage space for each child (e.g., cubbies, baskets, trays, desks) should be provided and labeled with children's names.

- An area for large group activities (usually a carpeted area where children can gather on the floor) should be provided.

- Space for small group activities (often large tables or several smaller tables pulled together) should be provided.

Every classroom space should be a center for learning.

- A place for individual quiet time (often separated from the high-activity areas of the classroom) should be provided.

- Spaces for quiet work should be separated from spaces where louder and more physical activity are expected.

- Traffic lanes should be set up so that children (including those with disabilities) can move efficiently and safely among the activity spaces of the classroom.

The short answer to the "how will space be organized?" question is *for learning*. How that plays out in each classroom will be different. Attending to these rules of thumb will help new teachers think through their options without taking away their own creativity and good judgment.

Where will the learning happen?

The term **learning center** takes on a broad meaning in the classroom I am advocating. Every space in the new kindergarten classroom should be a center for learning. Places for all the kinds of teaching described in Chapter 3 should be included as space is organized. Traditional early childhood learning centers (e.g., socio-dramatic play, blocks, manipulatives, and art) are good places for children to learn together and for teachers to use incidental teaching strategies. Subject matter centers (e.g., math, reading, science, social studies) provide opportunities for incidental, thematic, and tactical teaching. Individual and small-group spaces—such as listening stations, computer stations, writing centers, and classroom libraries—also generate opportunities for incidental, thematic, and tactical teaching. Large-group meeting spaces where everyone can join as a group and spaces where smaller groups can meet with the teacher offer opportunities for direct teaching.

My point is that classroom space should be set up to meet the learning needs of the students. I don't think setting up learning centers around a large carpeted area is enough, and I certainly don't think sitting five- and six-year-olds at desks is enough. As I will discuss below, kindergartners need a variety of activities using a variety of teaching approaches. Space should accommodate the learning objectives and instructional approaches of the classroom. While "everywhere" is the answer to the "Where will the learning happen?" question, that does not mean that space is randomly organized in hopes that learning will somehow happen. When "to learn a little every day" is the goal, teachers design instruction so that all of the space available in the classroom facilitates the accomplishment of that goal.

Balancing the Presentation of Activities— Every Task Has a Purpose

I have provided whole chapters on curriculum and teaching, but what will children actually do in the new kindergarten? Organization and management of classrooms at any level have everything to do with what children spend their time doing. When teachers prepare well and provide a variety of tasks that engage children in the act of learning, disruptions are minimized. When teachers "shoot from the hip" and make children do busy work and other mindless activities, disruptions are inevitable. Curriculum and teaching strategies come together in the activities that make up the school day. This section describes the kinds of tasks that maximize children's opportunities to learn.

To start, please notice I didn't say that teachers should provide *fun* activities. It's fine with me if students see activities as fun, but the purpose of kindergarten is to learn, and every task ought to reflect that purpose. However, that doesn't mean this should be set up as a **learning versus fun** argument. I believe that learning is inherently gratifying—that powerful positive feelings are associated with knowing that learning is happening for you and your friends. But too many well-meaning kindergarten teachers seem to operate as if the ultimate criterion is how much fun their students are having. It is possible, of course, to establish having fun as the purpose of schooling, but I see learning as a much more powerful and important goal.

What will children do? One way to get a picture of how activities might be organized is to imagine one child going through a morning in kindergarten.

APPLICATIONS

It's fine with me if activities are perceived as fun by the students, but the purpose of kindergarten is to learn, and every task ought to reflect that purpose.

Imagine you are talking to a college student who is thinking about kindergarten teaching as a career. The student exclaims, "I think I will be a great teacher because I am always thinking of fun things to do with kindergartners!" What should you say in response? How can you help this person see that fun should not be the defining criterion for judging what ought to be happening in kindergarten?

Chapter 5 is a comprehensive example of a week's worth of kindergarten activities, and the next section of this chapter outlines a sample daily **classroom schedule.** What follows is a sequence of activities one child (a boy we'll call Marcus) might experience on a typical morning, demonstrating the kinds of tasks that address genuine curriculum content and use the continuum of teaching strategies described in earlier chapters.

At Marcus's school, breakfast is provided for children, and they line up in the bus hall after breakfast until school starts at 7:45. Marcus enters the room with his classmates and goes immediately to the rug in the front middle of the room, where he is greeted by his teacher, who is sitting in a rocking chair at the front of the group. Marcus listens as his teacher welcomes the children to school, then he reads along with his peers as his teacher leads them through the daily message she has written on a portable whiteboard. Next, his teacher asks Marcus and the others to think of how many people in their families wear glasses. Marcus answers "two" when it is his turn as the teacher goes through the roll. The teacher explains that the students will be writing about people in their families who wear glasses when they write in their journals later in the morning.

It's another student's turn to check the weather, and Marcus watches as she tells the class it's cloudy and cold, while the teacher adds cloudy and cold symbols to the weather graph. Marcus counts along as the class decides that there have been seven cloudy and ten cold days this month. He watches as the weather person observes that so far there have been more cold days than sunny days. Marcus watches as the calendar person finds the date and places it on the proper square, then he recites the days of the week in English and Spanish with the rest of the class.

At this point, the principal greets the students and makes some announcements over the intercom, and the children stand and recite the Pledge of Allegiance. Next, it's Marcus's turn to do the math problem of the day. His teacher has placed cutouts of two triangles on one side of her felt board and three on the other. Marcus finds the felt numerals that match each set and places them beneath the cutouts. With the teacher's help, he picks out the plus and equal signs and places them on the board to make an equation. The class counts with Marcus and the teacher to determine that there are five triangles in all, and Marcus finds the numeral five and places it at the end of the equation.

Next, Marcus listens as his teacher reads a story about a child with newly prescribed glasses. After the teacher leads a discussion of the story and how the little girl in the story felt when her friends made fun of her new glasses, she tells the students what they will be doing today.

At the end of this group time on the rug, Marcus is assigned to work with a classmate (Amy) to "read and write the room." Marcus is given a clipboard, pencil, and a sheet with five lines on which to write words found in the room. Amy has a pointer, and together they find five words. Amy spells the words as Marcus writes them on the lines. Once all the pairs have found and written their words, Amy and Marcus join the others on the rug and take their turn reading the words on their clipboard to the group. Marcus and the rest of the class are then sent to their assigned seats at tables on the other side of the room.

At the tables, Marcus and the rest of the class participate in a large-group lesson on ordinal counting. He listens as the teacher explains what ordinals are, how they work, and when they are used. He watches as she demonstrates ordinal counting of several different objects aligned in a sequence, and he and the rest of the class count with her as she presents several more examples. At one point, he takes the lead in determining the position of the red race car when his teacher places five cars of different colors in different orders for children to count. The teacher passes out sheets with five race cars in a line, and Marcus and his peers color the cars according to the teacher's verbal directions (color the second car blue, color the fifth car yellow, etc.). When Marcus starts to color the fourth car yellow, the teacher counts with him to determine that the last car is in the fifth position and should be colored yellow.

The group moves back to the rug, where they all sing and move to a song that the teacher plays on the class CD player. After this, the teacher reminds the children what centers are available, and they move to their center activities. Marcus chooses one of the six computer stations in the room. He clicks on a program for matching initial consonant sounds with pictures on the screen, and he works with this program for about ten minutes.

Then one of his classmates taps him on the shoulder and tells him to get his journal and join the teacher at a table where three other children are already working. At the table, the teacher asks Marcus how many people in his family wear glasses and who they are. She invites him to draw a picture of these individuals (his mother and his older sister) in his journal. When he's done, she asks him to tell her about what he drew. As he dictates, she writes across the page, "My mama and my sister wear glasses." After Marcus reads back what they have written, he is sent to find Angela and tell her it's her turn to write in her journal.

Marcus goes to the sociodramatic play center, where two girls are using the materials to create an imaginary optometrist's office. When he comes into the center, one of the children has him "sign" the book, then she shows him to a chair that faces an eye chart borrowed from the school nurse. The other child hands Marcus a round piece of cardboard and tells him to cover one eye and read the chart. As he is doing this, another boy enters the "office," and all three children tell him he has to sign the book. The four children continue playing for the next several minutes, reading the eye chart and looking in each other's eyes with the magnifying glass and penlight the teacher has placed at the center.

At 10:30, the teacher tells the children that they will have to clean up in five minutes, and at 10:35, the clean-up music starts. Marcus helps his friends put the optometry materials away, then washes his hands for lunch.

This example of one child's morning activity shows how various teaching strategies can be balanced as real curriculum is taught. Marcus experiences incidental teaching alone and in combination with other teaching strategies when the teacher scaffolds his attempts at completing the addition problem, helps him identify the fifth car, and works with him on his journal entry. The class has been studying eyeglasses and eye care, and Marcus engages in several activities organized around this theme (answering the roll, writing in his journal, and playing in the optometrist office). A number of tactical teaching strategies were also employed as Marcus worked through his morning. These included being grouped with another child and working in a small group, observing modeling and demonstrations by the teacher, experiencing coaching by the teacher, participating in a discussion, and practicing the use of a concept he had just been taught. Marcus experienced direct teaching when the teacher presented her lesson on ordinals.

Curriculum content that Marcus was exposed to in this three-hour period came from language arts (reading sight words and simple text, correspondence between spoken and written words, environmental print, letters of the alphabet, letter sound correspondence, handwriting, spelling, listening, and speaking); math (counting, graphing, comparing, ordinal counting, matching numerals with sets, and addition); science (observing, communicating, weather concepts); social studies (family, kinds of work, shared and unique characteristics); health and physical education (movement); and art and music (creating art and performing music). Participating in this balanced set of activities made it possible for Marcus to learn more than a little on this day. I expect he had fun, but the point is that he learned. Marcus's teacher planned activities that used a variety of teaching strategies and addressed a broad spectrum of curriculum content. Every task had a purpose, and every activity added something to the children's learning experience. What will children do in the new kindergarten? They will learn real content in a variety of meaningful, engaging ways.

Balancing the Organization of Time— Every Minute Has a Purpose

Text books like this usually include a sample schedule, and I have done the same (see Figure 4.3). However, such a sample is only useful because it gives new teachers a framework for thinking about how to organize time. The realities of teaching in public schools, especially those that serve children who qualify for special education services and/or other programs supported by state and federal funds, are that children are often moving in and out of the classroom to go to resource, ESL, Title I, or speech classes. In addition, many kindergartens are served by **special areas** teachers for instruction in physical education, music, art, library, and guidance. These programs offer a great deal of support, but they have to be scheduled into the kindergarten day, and that means that the neat-looking schedules found in textbooks will have to be modified to meet the special circumstances found in virtually all schools. I have built in 30 minutes as a placeholder for special areas, but since individual children or small groups use the other special services, teachers will have to accommodate those interruptions on a case-by-case basis.

7:45	Opening Exercises
8:05	Large Group Instruction
8:40	Special Areas
9:10	Center Time and Small Group Instruction
10:30	Clean-Up and Prepare for Lunch
10:40	Lunch
11:10	Outdoor Play Time
11:40	Quiet Story Time
12:00	Large Group Instruction
12:30	Center Time and Small Group Instruction
1:10	Clean-Up and Prepare to Dismiss
1:20	Closing Exercises
1:30	Dismissal

Figure 4.3 | Sample Kindergarten Schedule

As with every dimension of kindergarten management and organization, decisions about time must be connected to maximizing learning opportunities. This is not the same as the obsessive concern with time on task that dominates some approaches to reforming early schooling. There are those who would take away outdoor play or center time because these activities take time away from the kind of school work some believe improves student achievement (i.e., scores on standardized tests). In classrooms where learning (not a narrow definition of achievement) drives everything that happens, time is important because it is a scarce commodity. Because there's only so much time available, it must be used in ways that tell children that every minute is a precious opportunity to learn. It's a feeling in the classroom that cannot be expressed in a written schedule. In fact, the time between activities and during transitions can be some of the most important learning time of the day. Routines and transitions are discussed below.

The framework represented in the sample schedule balances high-energy activities with quiet times, and acknowledges the need to be flexible in relation to the multiple contexts in which kindergarten happens. Teachers should make general modifications and specific adjustments based on their own schools, communities, classrooms, and students.

The sample schedule is based on a **modified, full-day kindergarten.** Children come to school at the same time as the other students in the elementary school, but leave an hour or so earlier. Many kindergartens continue to be set up in two half days and some have moved to the same schedule as the rest of the school, but the basic elements can be adjusted to fit the available time. Brief descriptions of the elements included in the schedule are presented here, then the importance of routines and transitions is discussed.

A Typical schedule

Opening exercises
Opening exercises signal the official start of the day by bringing children together in a large group. They involve such tasks as taking the roll, doing the calendar, checking the weather, reviewing where the class is in relation to ongoing thematic work, practicing newly acquired skills, orienting students to the day, telling students about new activities in learning centers, reading stories, singing songs, and doing movement activities.

Large-group instruction
Next is time for using teaching strategies that work best with the whole group. It is a time for introducing new skills and concepts that can best be taught

with teacher-directed activities, and it allows time for children to practice the new material so that the teacher can give immediate feedback and reteach where necessary.

Special areas

Physical education, library, music, art, and guidance are a part of many kindergarten schedules. A common pattern is for kindergartens to have each special area offered once per week. In some schools, these occur at a set time each day. In most schools, each day looks different, depending on when each special area is scheduled.

Center time and small-group instruction

During center time and small-group instruction, many activities can be going on at the same time. Learning centers based on thematic studies and/or special content are available. Content addresses the full range of the curriculum, and teachers use this time to work with small groups or individual children, implementing strategies from across the teaching continuum.

Clean-up and prepare for lunch

Next children put away the materials used during the preceding activity period and prepare for lunch: washing their hands, picking up their lunch boxes, getting meal tickets and money, lining up, and moving to the lunchroom.

Lunch

Lunch is frequently served early in the day for kindergartners, especially in large schools with many classes at each grade level. I preferred to eat with my classes when I taught, but others see this as an opportunity to associate with colleagues in an adult setting. In any case, lunchtime provides many important learning opportunities. Children learn how to interact in informal settings and to respect the rights of others. I always encouraged my students to behave in the lunchroom the same way they would in other public eating places. For example, people don't sit in silence in a restaurant, but neither do they shout or jump up and down because that would keep others from enjoying their meals.

Outdoor playtime

Play time should be made available daily, outdoors whenever the weather and facilities allow it. In some schools, playground time is controlled so that teachers have to plan around a master schedule. It is worth noting that I would move outdoor playtime to later in the day if I were teaching in a kindergarten pro-

Lunchtime provides many important learning opportunities.

gram that ran the full length of the elementary school day. Again, I wanted to be on the playground with my students because so many opportunities for social and physical skill development were available. I sometimes planned games and other movement-related activities, but usually left time for the children to play and enjoy each other, while I used incidental and tactical teaching strategies to help children learn and develop.

Quiet story time

This makes a nice transition from outdoor play (or lunch) back into the classroom. With some groups, I built in a short rest period, in which children could put their heads down and listen to soft music with the lights low. With all groups, I read a story for pleasure (without stopping to teach skills or strengthen comprehension). I often incorporated reading chapter books during this quiet period.

Large-group instruction, center time, and small-group instruction

After a quiet period, new material can be introduced in large group, but depending on what is being taught, activities from the earlier session might continue or alternatives might be added.

Clean-up and prepare to dismiss

It is now time to get the room back in order after a day's work and prepare to leave school. Kindergartners need time to get their backpacks together and, in climates where it's necessary, put on their coats and other gear. This is the time to distribute materials that need to go home and to be sure that everyone has all of his/her things. I like to get all this done before having a short closure activity, in order to avoid the chaos that often accompanies last-minute searches for lost gloves and so on.

Closing exercises

Closing exercises offer an opportunity to review the day. It is important to recall what was accomplished and to reflect on individual learning. I often asked each child to mention one thing that he/she learned that day, and I participated by talking about something that I had learned. This is also a good time to reorient children to where they are in their thematic studies and to foreshadow what's coming tomorrow and in the days ahead.

Dismissal

In my experience, dismissal is never just saying good-bye and sending children out the door. Routines for getting bus children to the right place, afterschool program kids to their spots, and car riders to their cars have to be well planned and consistently executed. Young children need to know that their transition out of school each day is well organized and safe. I made certain I had the chance to say something to each child as we parted so that we all left with a good feeling about the day.

The importance of the schedule

Dismissal is a good example of the importance of having well-planned **routines** for children and adults to follow during **transitions.** Transitions can become chaotic without careful planning, and children need to learn and practice the routines that make transitions run smoothly. Young children are not good at standing in lines, waiting, or keeping quiet. At some level, it is part of school life to stand in line, wait, and keep quiet; but to set up situations in which accomplishing these difficult tasks becomes the point is foolish and unnecessary. Better to move from one activity or location to another as smoothly and efficiently as possible, so children can learn to participate in making transitions work. Children need to learn how to move from large group instruction to center time, from the classroom to the cafeteria, and from special areas back into the classroom. I am sometimes amazed when teachers expect kindergartners to accomplish transitions without instruction and practice. It takes time, consistency, and repetition to get transitions to where they are routine. Without this investment, transitions can eat up time and energy that should be spent on learning.

I always had an activity ready whenever the inevitable occasions for waiting and keeping quiet in line arose. Simple activities that engaged children in singing, reciting, or practicing skills (e.g., skip counting down the line, thinking of objects that start with the first letters of their names, or making silly rhymes) made waiting time go faster and avoided the hassles of trying to "control" the class.

Transition routines have identifiable steps that can be learned and practiced, but children can also learn other procedures that make the day run more smoothly and help maximize their opportunities to learn. Procedures for going to the restroom, asking for help, and working at centers are examples. Early in the year is the time to help kindergartners learn routines and procedures, so wise teachers think through the routines and procedures they will use, they plan time to work on them with students, and they understand that not all children will catch on right away. It's a good idea to help children see the connections between the class rules and classroom routines and procedures. Routines and procedures are in place because they support the class objective that everyone will learn and support the learning of everyone else. When routines and procedures are not followed, valuable time is wasted and class rules that protect everyone's right to feel comfortable and learn are jeopardized. We want children to feel responsible for their behavior because it has a direct impact on how well the class operates as a learning community. So routines and procedures have value, not for their own sake, but because they maximize learning opportunities for everyone.

Balancing Assessment—Learn a Little Every Day and Make a Record of What Was Learned

Assessment

Assessment is a tricky issue in the new kindergarten. As was discussed in Chapter 1, accountability is a pervasive force in contemporary schooling, and its effects are being pushed down into early childhood classrooms. Almost all kindergarten teachers are being pressed to demonstrate that their students are learning a specified set of objectives, and the ways that learning is documented is more and more prescribed by forces outside the classroom. So no matter the teachers' personal preferences or professional beliefs, some of the assessment that goes on in kindergarten will likely involve giving children tests, having them complete prescribed evaluation activities, and/or observing their behavior based on a standardized checklist. I take this as a given in the current climate, but I don't see this as sufficient for providing a balanced program.

Assessment ought to improve teaching and learning in the classroom. It's an essential element in making sure children are learning all they can every day. My approach is to use the standardized assessment measures prescribed by systems, textbook publishers, and government agencies as diagnostic as well as evaluative tools. I think good teachers do this instinctively; that is, they reflect on how they can better reach each student as they grade tests, put children through assessment activities, or fill in checklists. But that by itself is not enough because what gets measured on these assessments is only a part of what children are learning, and the ways these assessments are set up limit what it's possible to learn about what children know and can do. Other assessment practices designed by the teacher are needed to balance the standardized tools imposed by someone else.

My approach to designing assessment practices is based on my assumption that content, ways to teach, and ways to figure out whether learning happened ought to be inseparably linked. If teachers have a clear idea of what they want to teach and how they want to teach it, then finding out whether kids are learning should follow naturally. For me, it's as simple as figuring out what you want children to be able to do, teaching them how to do it, then asking them to do it while you collect evidence on how well they do. Assessment needn't be a separate, sterile, or threatening exercise that takes place apart from the teaching and learning process. It should be built into every learning experience and provide opportunities for feedback and reteaching on the spot.

Vygotsky's (1978) notions of how children learn are especially valuable in implementing assessment designs for the new kindergarten. Berk and Winsler (1995, pp. 136–140) describe Vygotsky-inspired **dynamic assessment** procedures that stand in stark contrast to the static, standardized methods usually used to evaluate children's progress. Dynamic assessment situations are set up to determine not only what children can do on their own, but to find out what they can do with assistance, and what kind of assistance works best for them. So, if we're linking curriculum, teaching, and assessment, it makes sense to see assessment as an opportunity to find out whether the student has learned the

APPLICATIONS

Learn a little every day and keep a record of what's learned.

Imagine that the parents of one of your kindergartners are worried about the academic progress of their child. They have some concerns about your teaching methods, and they are unwilling to wait until the end-of-year tests to find out whether you are being effective. They have made an appointment to talk with you, and they are planning to speak to the principal as well. Plan what you will say and what you will bring to this conference. Take seriously their concerns about their child's academic progress as measured on standardized tests. Outline what you will say, and list what materials you will collect in preparation for this meeting.

content at an independent level, whether s/he can demonstrate competence with the assistance of the teacher, and what kind of scaffolding works best to assist the student who cannot do the task without assistance. Within this dynamic approach, assessment time is hard to distinguish from learning time, and the outcomes from the experience include information about independent development, potential development, and best ways to support future development.

Documentation

Learn a little every day and keep a record of what was learned. In order for teachers to make this happen, they need systematic ways to keep track of what's being learned. Assessment provides invaluable diagnostic information about what children need and the best ways to teach them. This information needs to be documented for the teachers' use, and as a record that parents, administrators, other teachers, and the children themselves may need or want. **Documentation** can involve building portfolios, taking photographs, writing anecdotal records, creating work folders, making audio and video recordings, and keeping learning journals. Early childhood education has a strong history of using child observation as a tool for developing curriculum and making instructional decisions. But there is evidence that traditional child observation is being eroded by accountability pressures (Hatch & Grieshaber, 2002). This is another place where trying for a balance is preferable to going overboard on either extreme. Standardized measures will not go away, so we should do our best to ensure

Teachers should document all they can about what children can do with and without adult support.

that they are used to support children's learning. At the same time, we should document all we can about what children can do with and without our support so we can maximize their chances of being successful learners.

Balancing Differences in Children's Abilities— Including All Children in the Learning Process

Dynamic assessment done right leads directly to tailoring experiences to the learning needs of individual children. When children demonstrate that they can perform certain skills or apply certain concepts when the teacher scaffolds their learning in certain ways, that teacher learns what those children need and how best to help them. This is true for all the children in the classroom, from the most to the least able. In fact, all the processes described in this book are designed to be adaptable for all kindergarten children, including children with disabilities.

For the past decade, I have worked with a terrific set of colleagues in the Inclusive Early Childhood Education Program to prepare early childhood teachers to work in inclusive settings. We set out to change the way "regular" education teachers were prepared by explicitly focusing on learning to teach in settings that included young children with disabilities. After all, it's the law that children with disabilities be placed in least-restrictive environments, and this usually means regular classrooms. Our approach, and the approach in this book, is that **inclusion** is not just a legal necessity, it provides advantages that benefit children both with and without disabilities. Just because it is right and beneficial to children does not make it easy. But applying the basic principles and practices in this book and adapting them to meet the special needs of children with disabilities will make it possible to balance the needs of everyone in your classroom.

The goal of learning a little every day is just as important for potentially gifted children as for those with identified or suspected disabilities. In the Inclusive Early Childhood Education Program, we helped prospective teachers get past the notion that teaching children with disabilities is a problem to be avoided if possible. Yes, it's a challenge, but meeting challenges is part and parcel of being a teacher, and we are proud of the quality teachers we have sent out to make a difference for all the children in their classrooms.

In this section, I provide several examples of how the basic ideas presented throughout this book can be modified to work for all children. It's impossible to teach everything every kindergarten teacher needs to know about every disability he or she might encounter, but it is possible to create a mindset and provide ways of thinking that support new teachers in inclusive classrooms. Many young children with disabilities come to kindergarten without having been identified by the special education system. Many school systems are rightly concerned about putting children through the special education assessment system before they have had a chance to mature and adjust to the school setting. This means that kindergarten teachers may have just as many children with disabilities in their classes as upper-grade teachers, but have fewer identified as such. From the perspective I am advocating here, that is not a critical distinction. All children are in kindergarten to learn, and it's the teacher's job to ensure that learning happens. A big part of that job is figuring out how best to teach each child, and while the solutions might be different for children with disabilities, the processes and overarching goals are the same. The descriptions that follow provide examples of alternative solutions within the framework of this book.

I have organized the discussions around categories of disabilities that kindergarten teachers are likely to see in their classrooms. For each area of disability, I describe general modifications and specific teaching adaptations that model the kind of thinking I am advocating here. Again, the point is not to list all the adjustments that need to be made for every curriculum goal and every disability; but to give new teachers a sense of how modifications for children with disabilities can fit comfortably within what they do for all children.

Hearing impairments

Children with hearing impairments benefit from being physically close to teachers and having teachers talk directly to them. Directions should be given clearly in a normal tone of voice after the child's attention has been gained. Opportunities for teacher-child and child-child communication should be maximized. The use of any assistive technologies (hearing aids, augmented speech devices) should be supported by teachers and child peers so that their benefits can be optimized.

Depending on the severity of the hearing loss, some children's learning will be enhanced if teachers and other children in the class learn some basic sign language. This can be a terrific experience for all concerned.

In terms of teaching strategies, the success of children with hearing impairments may be enhanced through incidental teaching in which the teacher (or a more advanced peer) scaffolds the child's learning in face-to-face interactions. Tactical teaching strategies that include small-group instruction, modeling and demonstrating, coaching, and tutoring are also likely to be successful.

In addition, some activities can be modified so that children with hearing difficulties can participate fully by using their other senses. For example, directions for center activities can be put on task cards that include pictures or combinations of words and pictures; finger spelling can be taught as new letters of the alphabet are introduced; finger-spelling charts can supplement the traditional alphabet letters displayed in the room; and visual cues (e.g., feltboard characters) can accompany oral explanations and demonstrations in large and small groups.

Visual impairments

Children with visual impairments need to feel secure in their environment, so the teacher should carefully orient them to how the classroom is organized and take particular care when physical changes occur. Depending on the severity of the child's impairment, several technologies, from simple magnifying systems to complex electronic devices that read text, are available to assist children in the classroom, and teachers need to know enough about these to be sure they are working and used to their fullest potential.

General modifications include being sure teachers produce text clearly and large enough for partially-sighted children to see, making sure children are close to them and/or the tasks at hand, and assigning peers to help children with visual impairments negotiate the day. As with hearing impairments, children with visual difficulties will benefit from face-to-face interactions with teachers and peers, strategies that allow for direct contact and thoughtful scaffolding, and opportunities to use their other senses to complete classroom tasks. Some examples of specific modifications include tape recording directions to activities at learning centers, using sand or salt trays to help children identify and write letters and numerals, and providing real objects that can be manipulated for teaching skills such as identifying likenesses and differences, classification, seriation, and patterning.

Physical impairments

Physical impairments can range from poor balance and coordination to needing a wheelchair or having very little fine or gross motor control. Obviously, moving through the spaces of the classroom is a first concern, as is having furniture that is suitable or adaptable for children who need accommodation. Again, wonderful assistive technologies have been developed to support children's learning, and these should be used effectively. When a child's impairment is strictly physical, the kinds of teaching used should not be limited except by the physical exigencies of the setting. That is, any strategy along the teaching continuum presented in Chapter 3 should be fine. Children with physical impairments may need support moving from place to place, collecting and using materials, and/or expressing their answers in written form, but unless they have multiple disabilities (which they sometimes do), their learning needs should closely match those of the other children in the kindergarten.

When multiple impairments are present, modifications described in other sections will come into play. Some specific modifications for children with physical impairments include placing learning center materials on tables high enough to accommodate a wheelchair, providing an older student or volunteer to take dictation when written answers are required, and altering movement and physical activities so that everyone participates.

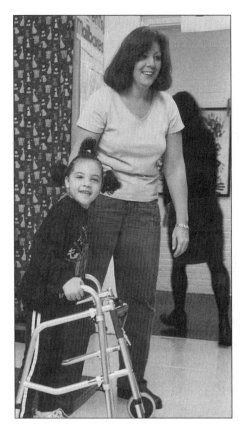

Including children with disabilities in regular kindergartens provides advantages that benefit children both with and without disabilities.

Emotional and behavioral impairments

Children with emotional or behavioral impairments are often the most challenging students for teachers at any grade level. This group can range from children who are diagnosed with attention deficit hyperactivity disorder (ADHD) to those identified as autistic. Behaviors can run from open defiance to total passivity.

General classroom characteristics that promote learning for children with emotional or behavioral impairments include creating and keeping predictable routines, building in lots of monitoring and feedback, and communicating in clear and consistent ways. Tactical strategies and direct teaching approaches modified for individual or small-group work generally work best for children with disabilities of this type. Modeling, demonstrating, and coaching can be valuable tools for helping children express their emotions and manage their own behavior so that they (and their classmates) have the opportunity to learn. Direct instruction (in small groups or one-on-one) that breaks learning down into logical, sequential steps that are carefully taught and practiced with immediate feedback may facilitate learning for children with emotional or behavioral impairments.

Some examples of specific modifications include breaking assignments into smaller units and expecting children to spend less time on individual tasks, setting up behavior modification programs that reward children for accomplishing classroom tasks, and working closely with assistants and/or volunteers to provide support for children during all parts of the day.

Cognitive impairments

Children with cognitive impairments who have been identified for special education services are often classified as "developmentally delayed" at the kindergarten level. Young children who have not been involved with the special education system but are obviously having difficulties learning at the same pace and in the same ways as other children need modifications as much as those with officially identified disabilities.

General modifications include designing activities that require children to perform according to their capabilities, providing activities with the same learning objectives but requiring different levels of ability, and setting up a classroom community in which everyone's learning is valued and supported by everyone else.

Children with cognitive impairments will benefit when instruction is direct, incremental, and face-to-face. They need opportunities to learn, practice, and relearn with the direct support of teachers, other adults, and child tutors. They can participate in activities using all of the teaching strategies across the continuum, but they will need support, patience, and several repetitions to master new content. Some examples of specific modifications include assigning more advanced partners to children who need help completing learning center activities, modifying a sight word game so that children who are not ready to read sight words can practice identifying letters of the alphabet, and adjusting questioning techniques so that all children can make positive contributions to group discussions.

These ideas are just a few examples of what's possible. Suggestions for generating effective modifications for specific disabilities are plentiful. Well-written **individualized education programs** (IEPs) should include specific, individualized strategies; special education teachers and district specialists should be valuable resources for ideas and support; and several publications are available that include practical suggestions for appropriate modifications (Cook, Tessier, & Klein, 2000; Judge & Parette, 1998; Wolery & Wilbers, 1994). Vygotsky (1993) made it clear that it is not children's disabilities per se that limit their development so much as the limitations those disabilities place on their opportunities to participate in the activities through which others learn. Our goal as kindergarten teachers ought to be to provide all children with opportunities to learn and to expect that every child will need modifications within a consistent framework in order to maximize his/her chances for success.

Balancing Parent and Community Involvement— Reciprocal Relations as a Genuine Goal

"Whose school is it?" This is a question I often ask my students. Some argue that the school belongs to the state or the local school board, others say that schools ought to reflect the values of the communities they serve, and still others believe that schools are in place for children. Almost no one takes the position that teachers own the school, but when I look at how teachers act, it appears to me that many teachers operate as if the school belongs to them. Further, I get a much stronger sense of teacher ownership when I ask, "Whose classroom is it?" Teachers want and expect to have a great deal of professional autonomy behind the closed doors of their classrooms. I want that too, but I believe part of exercising professional autonomy is to bring parent and community input to bear on school and classroom decision making through developing genuine **reciprocal relationships.**

In NAEYC's revised position statement on developmentally appropriate practice. Bredekamp and Copple note that "reciprocal relations between teachers and families require mutual respect, cooperation, shared responsibility, and negotiation of conflicts toward achievement of shared goals" (1997, p. 22). I would extend this to include teachers, families, and communities, and emphasize learning as a shared goal that all stakeholders can buy into.

Developing truly reciprocal relations with parents and communities is an ambitious goal. In many school settings, relations are more adversarial than reciprocal. Many teachers and administrators are unwilling to share decision-making power with others, and many parents and community members see themselves as unwelcome or unqualified to participate in school settings. Parent involvement has often meant getting parents to do what teachers want them to do (e.g., send in supplies, volunteer in the classroom, come to parent-teacher conferences), and parent education has meant teaching parents to be what teachers want them to be (i.e., the kind of parents they have or are trying to be themselves). Little or no reciprocity is involved in these relationships. Communication is typically one-way—from teacher to parent—and parents who challenge the system by trying to have an active voice in their children's education are often treated with disdain by school personnel.

I have painted with a broad brush, and probably unfairly smeared many educators who work very hard to establish positive working relations with parents and community stakeholders. In fact, kindergarten teachers, as a group, are probably among the most welcoming to parents and concerned about building good relations with them. Still, reciprocal relationships are generally a long way from reality in most school settings, including kindergartens.

Teaching in the new kindergarten means doing everything possible to encourage reciprocal relations with parents and communities. It means knowing who children and families are away from school, where they live, work, shop, play, and worship, and what they care about. This means

- Inviting parents and community stakeholders (businesses, churches, organizations, elders, and neighborhood leaders) to participate in important decisions related to the classroom

 APPLICATIONS

Many parents and community members feel they are unwelcome or unqualified to participate in school settings.

Imagine that you teach kindergarten in a school that busses in children from outside the neighborhood of the school in order to meet a court-ordered desegregation plan. Many of the children who ride busses to school are on free or reduced lunch plans, and their parents frequently lack personal means of transportation or resources to afford public transportation. What are some strategies that you could use to help these parents become more involved in the education of their kindergartners? What are some ways to reduce the physical, psychological, and social barriers that may inhibit their participation in the life of the school?

- Actually using the input they provide when the invitation is accepted
- Establishing effective avenues that let others know that communication will travel in two directions
- Having and using tools for resolving conflicts that focus on helping children be better learners, rather than turning into power struggles that no one really wins
- Being a part of a community, not just doing a job.

There are many specific things kindergarten teachers can do to encourage reciprocal relationships. If teachers do not have some direct knowledge of their students, their families, and the communities they serve, they will find it difficult to establish genuine give-and-take relationships. Teachers need to get to know children, families, and communities by having experiences with them. This means taking advantage of every opportunity at school to have positive social contact, but it also means getting out to where people live and meeting relevant stakeholders on their own turf. It sends a powerful message when

Reciprocal relations with parents depend on teachers having direct knowledge of their students, their students' families, and the communities they serve.

teachers visit homes, participate in neighborhood celebrations, visit local institutions, and attend important community events. In our teacher education program, we have prospective teachers do **community mapping** exercises that encourage them to find out all they can about the families and communities served by the schools in which they work (Benner & McLaughlin, 2003; Kretzmann & McKnight, 1993). They gather information directly from community stakeholders and develop complex understandings about the contexts of their students' lives that help them teach better and improve relations with parents and other community stakeholders.

To form partnerships for children's learning, teachers have to be willing to be partners and to let others know about that willingness. This starts with saying words like, "I want to find out what you want for your child" or "I want to find out what you want for the children in your community." How teachers listen and what they do with the information they get sets the tone for future interactions. As a graduate student, I was fascinated with Goffman's (1959, 1967) sociology of impression management and self-presentation. I learned that all communication happens on at two levels—the substantive (the substance of what is actually said) and the ceremonial (the expression of self that is included in how things are said) (Goffman, 1967). Relationships of all types are created at both levels. Teachers who want reciprocal relationships need to acknowledge an understanding of the substance that parents and others are communicating, but maybe more importantly, they need to value the integrity and legitimacy of the individuals making the statements. The ways teachers make eye contact, their body language, how they modulate their voices, and the way they shape their words send powerful messages about what they really want from potential partners. Unless they are accomplished actors, it will be impossible for teachers to fake ceremonial communications that send a message of respect and caring, but if they are committed to making meaningful connections with others, that message will come through.

Teachers who strive for reciprocal relations develop multiple avenues for two-way communication with parents (I use the term "parents" to stand for all those responsible for caring for the children away from the classroom). Weekly newsletters can keep parents informed about what was happening in kindergarten. But this practice by itself can send the message that communication is one way: from teacher to home.

Other tools should be used to keep communication flowing both ways. For example, the newsletter can include the opportunity for parents to respond by building in a regular reaction/concerns section or by asking specific questions on which teachers are seeking feedback. Another idea is to create take-home packets, often around the reading of a storybook, in which parents write with their children about their experience reading the book or completing another activity that parents are encouraged to do with their children. The packet can circulate so that parents can see what others have written. Writing interactive journals is another idea that connects teachers and parents. Such journals give parents and teachers a chance to write back and forth about the learning and development of individual children. In some schools, much of this kind of written interaction could take place on the Internet.

When parents are uncomfortable with or unable to participate in written communication, face-to-face and/or telephone contact is important. A simple commitment on the part of teachers to have positive contact with each parent on a regular basis avoids the worst case scenario of only talking with parents when problems arise. When contact is restricted to dealing with problems, reciprocal relations will be impossible. In the next section of this chapter, I discuss things to do when conflicts with parents and other stakeholders arise.

Active two-way communication is necessary for reciprocal relationships, but by itself, it is not sufficient. Reciprocity means sharing information *and power*. Unless stakeholders actually contribute to decisions, relationships exemplify a kind of pseudo-reciprocity. I have seen this in schools where parent advisory boards are formed, but their input is not seriously sought and their participation is mostly symbolic. Real reciprocal relations mean real input is sought concerning real issues, and real action is taken based on what parents and community representatives suggest. This does not mean capitulating to unreasonable demands; it does mean balancing perspectives so that it's clear that all stakeholders own the school and have an investment in what happens there.

Keeping Your Balance—Dealing with Threats to Classroom Equilibrium

Classrooms are complex, dynamic places that can never be in perfect balance. Keeping things as balanced as possible involves constant awareness of changing conditions in all the areas described in this chapter. It means not expecting that everything will be perfect and making adjustments based on maximizing everyone's opportunity to learn. In Chapter 3, I presented a problem-solving model that includes useful elements for making adjustments when problems arise. Here, I review those elements, then give a detailed example of using the model as a framework for restoring balance when classroom equilibrium is jeopardized.

APPLICATIONS

The short answer to "How do I restore classroom balance?" is "Whatever it takes."

Imagine that you are hired as a kindergarten teacher in November, after school has been in session for three months. The teacher you are replacing had medical problems, and the classroom seems to be in chaos when you arrive on your first day. Make a plan for systematically moving the class in the direction of becoming a learning community. Knowing that it will take time to build a shared commitment to learning in the group, spell out the steps you will take to accomplish this goal.

The short answer to "how do I restore classroom balance?" is "whatever it takes." But that doesn't mean taking random, frenetic action. It means being systematic about understanding problems and thoughtful about generating and trying possible solutions. The problem-solving model presented in Chapter 3 provides a framework for systematic, thoughtful decision making. The steps in the model are:

1. Pull together what you know.
2. Analyze the situation from a variety of perspectives.
3. Identify the problem(s).
4. Brainstorm a variety of short- and long-term solutions.
5. Anticipate the consequences of each viable option.
6. Make a plan.
7. Take action.
8. Assess the effectiveness of your actions.

Working with children who are not taking responsibility for their actions is an issue that confronts teachers in virtually all classrooms. Let's use this issue to create a detailed example of applying the steps of the problem-solving framework. While it is awkward to apply the model to hypothetical situations because we cannot actually go through the processes involved, providing a concrete example of what the processes might look like should help you understand how to implement the model in real settings.

When children do not take responsibility for their own actions, the efficacy of the classroom learning community is challenged. If children do not follow the classroom rules, the purpose of the class (everyone learning) will be diffi-cult to accomplish. For the sake of example, let's say that one child, Maria, is not fully participating in the classroom community. She fully engages in only a few of the learning activities that are presented, and her constant movement around the room, her loud voice, and her aggressive interactions with the other children are disrupting the learning opportunities of her peers. Maria's teacher wants to pull together what she knows as the first step in dealing with this prob-lem. She asks questions like the following:

- What is Maria's history?
- Was Maria in preschool, family day care, or at home prior to starting kindergarten?
- What is Maria's family like?
- Who is responsible for taking care of Maria away from school?
- Where does Maria live?
- What is Maria's behavior like at home, in afterschool care, and in the neighborhood?
- Is there any history of medical problems?
- What does Maria's behavior look like in class?
- Are there certain behaviors that are repeated in a pattern?
- Are there times of day when Maria is more (or less) agitated?
- Are there activities in which Maria is more (or less) engaged?
- Are there certain children with whom Maria has more (or less) antago-nistic interactions?

In this step, the teacher wants to gather factual information that can be verified through records, direct observation, or questioning.

In the second step, the teacher wants to use the collected information to make sense of the problem from a variety of perspectives. She asks questions like:

- What are some explanations for why Maria cannot stay in one place?
- Why is Maria having problems remembering the rules?
- Why does Maria appear not to care that others are not learning when she disturbs them?
- Why is Maria so aggressive with her peers?
- What is going on from Maria's perspective?
- How might Maria's parents explain what is going on?

The goal in this step is not to find a definitive answer to the questions but to look at the issue from as many angles as possible. The key is to look to the information gathered in the first step as the source for possible answers at this stage. For example, knowing that Maria has never been in a classroom setting before, or that she has lived in three foster homes in the past two years, or that she has a history of chronic earaches will lead to different answers than might be generated from knowing that she attended Head Start, lives in a stable home, or has a history of perfect health. Further, knowing that she is least engaged when working with peers away from adult supervision, is most active in the morning, or is most aggressive with larger boys will lead to different possibilities than knowing that she works relatively well in small groups, seems agitated all day, or is really only aggressive in self-defense. The idea is to use the information to make some informed guesses about what is going on.

The third step is to identify the problem or problems. Here, the teacher uses her best professional judgment to select from the alternatives generated from completing the first two steps. In steps two and three, an underlying question ought to be, "Whose problem is it?" We should not start with the assumption that the problem is in the child. It is shortsighted and ineffective to look for problems within children, their families, or their communities. And yet, listening to talk in teachers' lounges, one might think that all the problems that besiege schools fit these categories. Identifying problems in terms like "She's hyper," "Her parents don't care," or "Violence is a way of life in her neighborhood" is common because defining problems in these terms takes responsibility away from teachers and schools. After all, what can we do about any of these?

What I am suggesting is that factors related to children, their homes, and their lives away from school be understood and taken into account, but that problems be located as close to the classroom action as possible. In our example, while it's important to know that Maria has some symptoms of ADHD, the issue to be dealt with may be that she is being asked to behave in ways that she has never been taught. This makes it a problem that belongs to more than just Maria. For the sake of this discussion, I have generated several problem statements that serve as examples:

- Maria is being asked to behave in ways she has never been taught.
- Her peers are treating Maria as a less-than-normal outsider.
- Classroom activities are too easy/difficult for Maria.
- The classroom routine is too structured/flexible for Maria.
- Maria is spending too much/little time working with small groups.

- Teacher directions are not being heard/processed by Maria.
- The relationship between classroom rules and her behavior is not understood by Maria.
- Maria does not yet know what learning is and/or has not come to see herself as a learner.
- Maria does not feel safe/secure/cared for in the classroom setting.

The next step is to brainstorm a variety of possible short- and long-term solutions. As in step two, the goal in step four is to think inductively, generating as many possibilities for interventions as possible, while reserving judgment about the options until later. Staying with the example, let's say that the teacher decides that the central issues for Maria are that she does not feel safe and secure in the classroom and that she does not see the relationship between her behavior and the classroom rules. It's the teacher's judgment that Maria's feelings of being disconnected from her peers and her lack of understanding that what she does affects the learning of others are tied together. One problem feeds the other—when Maria breaks the rules, her peers reject her and Maria feels further alienated from the group and more likely to break the rules. A list of ideas for intervening in these interconnected problems might look like this:

- Plan role-playing activities that show how children feel when rejected by peers.
- Plan role-playing activities that show how others feel when rules protecting their rights are broken.
- Read children's literature about overcoming rejection and discuss how others feel when they are left out or put down.
- Set up activities so that Maria works with others who are adept at prosocial behavior and who see the purposes of the rules.
- Explain the rules and their purposes to Maria in a face-to-face meeting away from the other children.
- Review the rules and their purposes with the whole group and remind everyone of the consequences for the "learning team" when someone breaks the rules.
- Set up a coaching strategy that shows Maria the immediate consequences for the classroom community when rules are broken and that teaches alternative behaviors on the spot.

- Assign a socially competent peer to partner with Maria during difficult times of the day.
- Develop social studies activities that teach the importance of making everyone feel safe and secure in the classroom.
- Set up a behavior modification plan with Maria, rewarding her when she follows the rules and has positive relations with peers.
- Seek input and support from the school psychologist and/or guidance counselor.
- Consult with Maria's parents to gather input on their perspective and possible suggestions for classroom strategies.
- Make sure Maria is getting her turn at classroom jobs that require responsibility and leadership.

The fifth step is to study the potential intervention ideas and anticipate the consequences of each viable option. Some ideas that come up during brainstorming may not be feasible, given the constraints of time and resources. In our example, it may be that the demands of working with 15 other children who also have high needs preclude the teacher's implementation of a coaching strategy or that access to psychological services for kindergartners is unavailable in Maria's school system. Some interventions that may be good ideas for most children will not work with the particular child in question. For example, having Maria partner with another child may create more problems than it solves. Other potential solutions may have unintended consequences that make their usefulness limited. For example, some children in Maria's class might learn the wrong lessons from role-playing activities, coming away believing that Maria or others like her deserve to be excluded and ostracized. The intent of this step is to analyze what you think will happen if you decide to try each step. The process of doing the analysis will likely lead to adding ideas or modifying ones already on the brainstormed list. The final result will be a set of viable strategies that will form the basis for your plan.

Making a plan (step six) means taking the information from step five and putting together a sequence of short- and long-term actions for addressing the problem. It is important to be as specific as possible about what you will do and when you will do it. Good intentions and nebulous plans with unspecified timelines do not restore balance when genuine problems exist. An example plan for working with Maria might look like this:

- First Tuesday: Have Maria stay behind when children go to music and speak to Maria privately. Remind Maria of the important place of learning in the classroom, go over the rules and their relationship to everyone's learning, use specific examples of Maria's recent behavior to show how they disrupted her and others' chances to learn, and discuss alternative behaviors that would fit the rules and meet the purposes. Stress the importance of belonging to the learning team, ask her what she thinks will help her participate more effectively, and send the message that you will support her efforts to learn and help others learn.

- Three weeks: Follow up this meeting with daily one-on-one reminders, feedback, and reinforcement when behaviors fit classroom purposes.

- First Friday and ongoing for three weeks: Block some time during opening exercises to review the rules and their purposes with the whole group. Remind everyone of the consequences for the "learning team" when someone breaks the rules. Do not single out Maria, but emphasize that everyone is a learner and everyone is responsible for helping others learn a little every day.

- Next week and ongoing: Review instructional plans, looking for opportunities to team Maria with children who are prosocial in the classroom. Select children who are adept at making positive contact with others, monitoring the effects of their behavior on those around them, and adjusting to the behavior of others. Some opportunities might involve forming ad hoc groups to complete art activities, putting specific children together in learning centers, or creating groups for project work.

- Within ten days and ongoing: Ask the media specialist to collect children's literature about dealing with rejection, and read one selection per week for the next several weeks. As books are shared, help children discuss how they feel when they are left out or put down by others, and talk about ways they could help children who are stigmatized by their peers.

- In three weeks (if needed): Set up an appointment with Maria's parents to explain what's going on and gather input on their perspective and suggestions for potential classroom strategies. Frame the discussion around finding ways to maximize Maria's opportunities to learn and participate positively in the learning of others.

- Ongoing: Develop an integrated theme study around social studies content related to rules and responsibilities, focusing on activities that teach the importance of making everyone feel safe and secure in the classroom.

- Fourth week and ongoing: Set up a behavior modification plan with Maria, breaking the day into small segments, identifying behaviors that are desirable for those segments, and rewarding her when she exhibits those behaviors.

Step seven is taking action—the implementation of your plan. Just do it and keep track of what you did. It is important to make a record for yourself of exactly what you did and when. These records could also become important later on as decisions about future interventions and/or special education evaluations are made. But most importantly, you need to be able to look at what you have done in order to complete the next step, assessing the effectiveness of your actions.

Solving classroom problems is a process that requires teachers to gather information about how well their attempts are working. Unless this step is included, teachers will never know what worked and what didn't. In the example, it will be important to assess effectiveness after the short-term strategies have had a chance to work (about three weeks in) to see if the longer-term alternatives will be needed and at what level. Further, in all situations in which this model is applied, it is likely that assessment at the end will lead to further modifications to the plan and a renewed effort based on the information gathered during the process.

Closing Thoughts

It is important for teachers to bring balance to their work with kindergarten children, their families, and their communities. I honestly don't know how this can be done in any meaningful way unless teachers are committed to some purpose for their work. In terms borrowed from elementary physics, a purpose provides the fulcrum for the balance. Without a fulcrum, the notion of balance has no meaning. I prefer learning as the purpose for kindergarten (and all schooling), but, as mentioned above, others are possible.

Whatever the purpose, kindergarten teaching done well will not be easy. The fulcrum might change, but the necessity of balancing the complex elements discussed in this chapter will always be there. In the final chapter of this book, I present a detailed example of a full week of kindergarten instruction in a classroom that values learning as the fulcrum of schooling and that applies the curricular and instructional approaches presented in this book to demonstrate how children can learn a little every day.

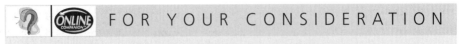

FOR YOUR CONSIDERATION

1. What would kindergartens be like if everyone agreed that mastering the competencies measured on standardized achievement tests was the purpose of school?

2. What are the advantages and disadvantages of classroom management systems based on rewards and punishments?

3. What are the pros and cons of universal full-day kindergartens?

4. What supports and obstacles work for and against including children with disabilities in regular kindergarten classrooms?

5. What is your answer when someone asks, "Whose school is it?"

LEARNING ACTIVITIES

INDIVIDUAL ACTIVITIES

- Study how space is used in several kindergarten classrooms. Keep track of different physical arrangements, and analyze what spaces are used for and who appears to own them.

- Write a letter to the parents of an imaginary kindergarten class explaining that a child with autism will be included in your classroom. Emphasize the benefits you see for both the child with autism and the other children in the class.

SMALL GROUP ACTIVITIES

- Work together to construct a questionnaire that you could send to parents, asking them to provide information about their entering kindergartners. Have parents you know review your questionnaire and give you feedback about the form and content before completing a final draft.

- Compare the classroom schedule in this chapter with schedules from other textbooks, district curriculum guides, and/or schedules from real kindergarten teachers. Analyze what's the same and different across schedules, then construct a classroom schedule based on your group's preferences and experiences.

Continues

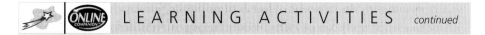

LEARNING ACTIVITIES *continued*

LARGE GROUP ACTIVITIES

- Invite a group of parents of young children with disabilities to talk with the class. Ask parents to describe their children and tell what they would like their children to experience in kindergarten. Encourage students to prepare thoughtful questions in advance of the parents' visit.

- Discuss what qualities would move college classes to becoming communities of learners. Identify classroom rules that would encourage the expression of those qualities in the classroom. Post the rules and refer to the rules when appropriate.

CHAPTER 5

What Will a Week Look Like in a New Kindergarten Classroom?

T his chapter provides a comprehensive example of one week's instruction in kindergarten. The goal is to show new teachers how the ideas in this book can be integrated into a meaningful whole. Elements of curriculum from areas described in Chapter 2, examples of teaching strategies outlined in Chapter 3, and applications of principles presented in Chapter 4 are addressed within the week's description. The body of the chapter is organized around the daily schedule presented in Figure 4–1. Each day of the week is described from beginning to end and in enough detail to provide a snapshot of a new kindergarten in action.

I planned this week as if it were the third week in January. I selected this week because it is about midway through the year and approximately halfway through the curriculum. I imagined a class of 15 to 18 children from a variety of socioeconomic and cultural backgrounds. I planned for two children with learning difficulties (Dorene and Rod) and one child with fine- and gross-motor difficulties (Gina) that confined her to a wheelchair. I assumed that the classroom had adequate space and standard kindergarten furniture, equipment, and materials.

As I planned, I built in an integrated theme study on winter to demonstrate how thematic teaching can be used alongside incidental, tactical, and direct approaches. As I describe instructional activities, I identify the teaching strategies being employed by placing an identifier in brackets (e.g., [Tactical— Tutoring]). I highlight the curriculum content for each activity using italics inside parentheses (e.g., *Language Arts, Reading—Decoding*). These devices are designed to make it easy to see how curriculum, instruction, and classroom organization can be put together in a variety of ways.

Each school, each classroom, each group of students, and each teacher will be different

The description is just an example of what's possible. Each school, each classroom, each group of students, and each teacher will be different; so the best way to read the example is to look at the patterns of thinking that went on behind the decisions to teach certain content in certain ways under certain conditions.

Monday

7:45 Opening Exercises

The day begins on the carpet. Mrs. Allen greets her students and tells them that this week they will be studying one of the seasons. She asks who remembers the four seasons, then leads the group in reciting winter, spring, summer, and fall. She asks what season it is now, and tells them that they will be studying winter this week [Thematic—Integrated Thematic Study]. She picks up a marker and starts a K-W-L chart on winter, asking the children to name all the things they know (K) about winter. She records their responses on the chart, reviews what they have written, then starts another page on which she records what they tell her they want (W) to learn about winter [Tactical—Discussing] (*Language Arts, Writing—Dictated Messages and Stories*).

Next, she asks the child assigned as weather helper to go with her to the window to check the temperature on a large thermometer placed just outside. The helper reports the temperature and weather conditions to the class, and Mrs. Allen starts a record of daily temperatures on a chart she has prepared ahead of time (*Science, Earth and Space Science—Weather; Science Processes—Observation and Communication*). The school is in Vermont, so the teacher brings in a shallow pan in which she placed water the night before. The children discuss what happened (the water has frozen) and Mrs. Allen explains the freezing mark on a mock thermometer. She asks the students what will happen if the temperature goes above 32 degrees Fahrenheit later in the week. (The teacher could also freeze water in a refrigerator freezer and lead a discussion on the freezing point of water and what it means.) Children should have the opportunity to touch the ice and talk about how it looks and feels [Tactical—Discussing] (*Science, Physical Science—Matter; Earth and Space Science—Weather*).

Mrs. Allen next tells the children about activities related to winter that they will be doing this week. She points out new books in the reading center, winter clothing in the sociodramatic play center, playdough for making snowmen in the art center, and a snowflake-sorting activity in the theme center. She then introduces a new song about winter ("Dancing Snowflakes" to the tune of "Are You Sleeping?"). She sings the song and demonstrates the movements for them, then has them join in [Tactical—Demonstrating] (*Music—Performing Music; Physical Education—Movement*).

Opening exercise routines (calendar, days of the week, helpers chart) are then completed. Because this is the first day of the thematic study, opening exercises have run longer than usual and less time will be available for large-group instruction. Mrs. Allen sends the children to their assigned table spaces at the back of the classroom for an activity about the word "cold."

8:05 Large-Group Instruction

Mrs. Allen tells the children that they will be learning about the word family "old" today. She shows them the letters o-l-d and explains that they spell the word "old," and she reminds them that word families are words that end with the same letters. She gives them examples of word families they have already worked with ("at"—bat, cat, fat, hat; and "ill"—bill, fill, pill, will). She refers back to the K-W-L activity they did during opening exercises and reminds them that "cold" was one of their winter words, pointing out that "cold" is a member of the "old" word family. She next writes out several examples of "old" word family members (cold, fold, gold, hold, sold, told), emphasizing that they all end with "old" and that changing the initial consonant makes a new word.

She next passes out a worksheet on which "old" is written five times with a blank space before each one. She tells the children that she will name a word from the "old" family, and they will write the letter that starts that word on the proper blank. They do the first one together, then as they complete the other four, she circulates among the children, monitoring their work, giving feedback, and providing more instruction and support for those who don't get it or have trouble writing the letters. She concludes by asking them what they have just learned, leading them through a review of what word families are, how they work, and what words belong in the "old" family [Direct Teaching] (*Language Arts, Reading—Word Families; Writing—Upper- and Lowercase Letters*). She tells them that she will add the "old" family to the word family bulletin board so they can use it in their "read and write the room" activity later.

8:40 Special Areas

Mrs. Allen will have told special areas teachers about the class integrated thematic study of winter ahead of time, as well as provided them with a sample of the activities children would be doing in relation to each special area. Some special area teachers will be able (and willing) to connect with the theme and activities; others will not.

APPLICATIONS

Some special area teachers will be able (and willing) to connect with the theme and activities; others will not.

Imagine that you are planning a thematic unit on winter like the one in this chapter. You teach in a school that provides 30 minutes of library, physical education, music, and art instruction once per week for your kindergartners. Prepare a one-page note for each special area teacher that explains what you are doing, points out the advantages of connecting the theme and content covered to work in each special area, and offers examples of easy ways to connect the special activities to your winter theme.

9:10 Center Time and Small-Group Instruction

As children return from special areas, Mrs. Allen holds a short planning meeting on the rug to get the children started in centers and small-group instruction. Again, she points out the new (fiction and nonfiction) books about winter in the reading center and tells them that winter clothing has been placed in sociodramatic play center. She shows them a snowman she has made from playdough in the art center and tells them they need to plan their time so that they can make a snowman today or tomorrow during center time (*Art—Creating Art*). She shows them the snowflake-sorting activity in the theme center and talks about different ways they can match, sort, and order the snowflakes when they go there (*Math, Algebra—Comparing and Sorting*). She reminds them that computers and the writing center will be open today as well.

Most children are sent to centers (where limits on the number of children who can use them are pre-established), and Mrs. Allen pulls groups of four or five children to join her back at one of the work tables [Tactical—Grouping]. Most children work on number words with the teacher as she uses flash cards to review number words to ten for some groups and to five for others, then leads

Opportunities for independent and small-group work should be made available during center time.

a matching game with numerals and number words. Some children, including Dorene and Rod, need more work on the concept of number and identifying numerals, so these children review these skills and play a game of matching domino dots with numerals (*Math, Number, and Operations—Concept of Number; Numerals; Number Words*).

Mrs. Allen builds in time to work with Gina at the art center. She shows Gina how to mold the playdough into balls and places her hands around Gina's to support her efforts. Mrs. Allen talks about making a larger ball for the base and two smaller balls for the body and head as she helps Gina put her snowman together [Tactical—Coaching]. Mrs. Allen also stops by the writing center where a child is writing words from the word wall. The boy is reversing his lowercase b's (writing them as d's), and Mrs. Allen points to the alphabet model in the center and reminds him he can look at the model to be sure which way the b faces. They write "bat" together to practice how it works [Incidental Teaching]. The teacher gives a five-minute warning to the group so that the children know a transition is coming.

10:30 Clean-Up and Prepare for Lunch

At 10:30, Mrs. Allen begins singing the clean-up song and circulates around the room to be sure everyone is putting the room back the way it was. Children are sent, by tables, to wash their hands. They pick up their lunches or lunch tickets and return to their assigned places before lining up to go to the lunchroom. Mrs. Allen tells the children they will be going for a walk after lunch to look for signs of winter.

10:40 Lunch

Mrs. Allen takes the children to the lunchroom, stays with them until they have filled their trays and been seated, then leaves them with the cafeteria assistants until she picks them up at 11:05.

11:10 Outdoor Play Time

The children put on their winter gear when they get back to the classroom, and Mrs. Allen tells them they will be going on a short field trip around the school campus to look for signs of winter. She reminds them to use all their senses to observe the world outside so they can write down everything they learn when they come back inside. Making sure the other children are helping Gina safely go wherever the class goes, teacher leads the group around the school grounds. She stops to help children focus on particular signs of winter such as dormant plants, leafless trees, brown grass, frozen puddles, snow patches, icicles, foot-prints in the snow, cold temperatures, seeing their breath, listening for bird-songs and insect noises, and the sounds of walking on the snow and ice (*Science, Earth and Space Science—Weather; Science Processes—Observation*).

11:40 Quiet Story Time

After the children put away their outdoor clothing, they come to the rug and Mrs. Allen introduces a book about a boy who went outside on a snowy winter day. She reminds them that they will be making an experience chart about their winter walk after the story and asks them to think about what they observed on their walk that was the same or different from what Peter, the boy in the story, saw when he was outside. She then shares *The Snowy Day* (Keats, 1962).

12:00 Large-Group Instruction

After reading *The Snowy Day*, Mrs. Allen starts an experience chart on which she records the children's observations from their winter walk [Tactical—Dis-cussion] (*Language Arts, Reading—Correspondence Between Spoken and Writ-ten Words; Writing—Dictating Messages and Stories*). She starts by letting them name signs of winter that they observed, then prompts their thinking by asking what they observed with their different senses. When the chart is complete, they read the chart together, and she picks up the book and asks what they have on their chart that Peter observed when he was outside. Using the book and their chart as sources of information, she also asks them to think of things that they observed that Peter did not in the story. The teacher includes a discussion of how winter is different in different places.

12:30 Center Time and Small-Group Instruction

The same centers will be available as in the morning, and Mrs. Allen reminds children of what's open and that (if they didn't do it this morning) they need to make a snowman this afternoon or tomorrow during center time. Mrs. Allen passes out multiple copies of *The Snowy Day* and leads children in small groups of four or five, in a search for uppercase letters and ending punctuation marks [Tactical—Grouping] (*Language Arts, Reading—Print Conventions*). In some groups, she reads all of the text on a page, asks children to find all the uppercase letters, then leads a discussion of why they are upper- instead of lower-case letters. For other groups, she reads most of the text, pausing in some places so children can join in the reading, then asks the children to find uppercase letters and ending punctuation marks. For one group, children do much more of the reading, and they too find and discuss uppercase letters and punctuation marks. In all groups, the children go through the story, focusing on certain print conventions. With the remaining time, Mrs. Allen circulates among the centers enjoying the children and scaffolding their learning.

1:10 Clean-Up and Prepare to Dismiss

After a five-minute warning, children clean up, put on their gear, collect their backpacks, lunchboxes, and other materials, and sit in their seats at the tables. Mrs. Allen sends home a newsletter every Monday, so she reviews this and passes it out to the children so they can put it in their backpacks along with school notices and other materials that need to go home.

1:20 Closing Exercises

Once they are settled, Mrs. Allen leads students in a review of the day. She asks each child to name one thing he/she learned today. She reminds them that they will continue studying winter tomorrow and the rest of the week, asks them to watch for other signs of winter, and mentions that on Friday they will be making something special to eat to celebrate the end of their winter study.

1:30 Dismissal

Tuesday

7:45 Opening Exercises

Opening exercises begin with a reminder that the theme study of winter will continue. Mrs. Allen calls the roll by asking each child to name one thing he/she remembers about winter from their work yesterday. She concludes this discussion by reading over the K-W-L chart from yesterday and reminding the children what they are learning and planning to learn.

Next she and the weather helper observe the temperature outside, check on the pan of water, and record the information on the chart. Together, the group compares the weather today with yesterday's weather and predicts what the weather will be tomorrow. Mrs. Allen uses the mock thermometer to review the freezing point of water as they discuss whether the water left outside froze overnight.

Mrs. Allen then reads a new story about winter, A *Walk on a Snowy Night* (Delton, 1982). She leads the children in a discussion of what elements of winter were in this story and helps them compare this story with the winter story from yesterday (*A Snowy Day*). She reminds them that the characters in both stories used their senses to learn about winter just like the class did yesterday on its walk around the school [Tactical—Discussion].

The class sings the "Dancing Snowflakes" song from yesterday, then completes the opening exercise routines (calendar, days of the week, helpers chart). During calendar time, Mrs. Allen reviews the names of the seasons and asks what season it is.

8:05 Large-Group Instruction

At the tables, Mrs. Allen tells the children that they will be learning about descriptive words. She explains that descriptive words are words that tell how things look, feel, taste, smell, and sound. She holds up a ball and names several words that tell how the ball looks (e.g., red, round, big). She shows them a cotton ball and tells them several words that describe how it feels (soft, fluffy, light). She shows a picture of pudding and names words that describe how it might taste (sweet, tangy, smooth). She follows the same procedures for a picture of a flower, giving descriptive words that tell how it might smell (sweet, strong, pretty), and finishes by ringing a bell and giving words to describe the sound (loud, noisy, pretty). Mrs. Allen tells the students that descriptive words help us tell others what the things we observe are like.

Then Mrs. Allen gives each child a small plastic bowl with an ice cube in it. She tells the children that they are going to think of descriptive words to help others understand what ice is like. She asks them to first think of words that tell how ice looks, and she records these on a chart. Staying close so she can work with Gina as needed, Mrs. Allen then has the children feel the ice and give her words for the chart that say how the ice feels. Then, for those who want to, she has the children taste the ice to describe how it feels and tastes in their mouths. She goes over the chart with the children reiterating how the words they have written describe ice [Direct Teaching] (*Language Arts, Reading—*

Direct instruction in large groups is an appropriate way to teach certain curriculum elements.

Correspondence Between Written and Spoken Language; Writing—Dictated Messages and Stories; Speaking—Descriptive Language).

8:40 Special Areas (Parallel to Monday)
9:10 Center Time and Small-Group Instruction

The same activities as Monday are available in the centers today. Mrs. Allen reminds the children what their choices are and that those who have not made a snowman or worked with the snowflake-sorting activity need to do so this morning or at afternoon center time. She tells them that she has placed copies of *The Snowy Day* in the listening center, so up to four children can listen to the story on tape as they follow along with the book.

Small-group instruction is focused on phonics. During this period, Mrs. Allen calls four groups to her table [Tactical—Grouping, Practicing]. The first two groups practice blending consonant-vowel-consonant (CVC) patterned words that have been previously introduced. Mrs. Allen reviews the short *a* and *i* vowel sounds with these groups, then writes CVC words on a chart (e.g., pat, man, sit, fig) and has the children blend the sounds together to figure out the words. She makes sure each child has a chance to sound out several words independently. For a third group, she includes all of the short vowel sounds in the CVC activity, plus she adds some nonsense syllables to the blending practice (e.g., fam, ped, rin, vot, nug). This is treated as word play to help them see the value of using their decoding skills to figure out unfamiliar words (*Language Arts, Reading—Decoding*). Dorene and Rod are called as the fourth group, and they work with Mrs. Allen on remembering and practicing the consonant sounds that have been introduced so far (*Language Arts, Reading—Letter-Sound Correspondence*).

10:30 Clean-Up and Prepare for Lunch (Parallel to Monday)
10:40 Lunch (Parallel to Monday)
11:10 Outdoor Play Time

Depending on the weather, the children will play outdoors in the designated area or have a period of movement activities in the classroom. Both indoors and out, Gina participates in all activities at whatever level she is able, and the children have learned to support her efforts spontaneously. Still, Mrs. Allen sometimes gives specific suggestions for how her peers can help Gina participate more fully.

11:40 Quiet Story Time

Mrs. Allen shares the big-book version of *The Mitten* (Brett, 1989) with the children, and she tells them that they will practice remembering what happened in the story during large-group time.

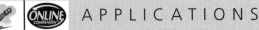

APPLICATIONS

Depending on the weather, the children will play outdoors in the designated area or have a period of movement activities in the classroom.

Imagine that you work in a school system that is thinking about doing away with recess. Outline what you would say to parents, administrators, and community leaders to help them see that play and movement are important for children in school.

12:00 Large-Group Instruction

Mrs. Allen tells the class that she will read *The Mitten* again. It will be their job to listen carefully and remember the order in which things happened in the story. She tells them that after she reads it one more time, they will retell the story together. As she reads the story again, Mrs. Allen prompts the children to remember the order of events in the story (a series of animals take shelter in a boy's lost mitten). After the second reading, Mrs. Allen helps the group retell the story in order, using the book to confirm their memories [Tactical—Discussion] (*Language Arts, Listening—Comprehension; Speaking—Story Retelling*).

12:30 Center Time and Small-Group Instruction

The same centers are open this afternoon as this morning. Mrs. Allen introduces some new sight words in four randomly organized small groups. In each group, she tells the children that they will be learning some new sight words, reminds them of what sight words are, and presents the new sight-word cards. One at a time, she reads the words, discusses what they mean, uses them in a sentence, and points out any distinguishing characteristics and/or shared features they have with words the children have already learned. The children practice reading the new words together, then Mrs. Allen flashes the cards, calling on individual children to read them and say what they mean or use them in a sentence. For individual children who are able, she flashes the new words in rapid-fire fashion [Direct Teaching] (*Language Arts, Reading—Sight Words*).

Between groups, Mrs. Allen visits the sociodramatic play area, where two children are dressing for winter. She sees Debby who appears to want to join the play, but is watching from nearby. Mrs. Allen asks Debby if she would like to play with the winter clothes too, and when she nods yes, Mrs. Allen suggests that she ask the children already in the center if she can play. When Debby appears reluctant, Mrs. Allen prompts her to say, "Can I play with you?" The child tries it with the teacher, then with her peers in the center, and she joins in the dress-up activity [Incidental Teaching].

1:10 Clean-Up and Prepare to Dismiss (Parallel to Monday)

1:20 Closing Exercises

After being sure everyone is ready for dismissal and after reviewing what they learned today, Mrs. Allen shows the children several examples of winter scenes from the books they have been reading and other books in the library center. She tells them that starting tomorrow they will be making a class mural of their own winter scene, so they should be thinking about what they would like to paint onto the mural.

1:30 Dismissal

Wednesday

7:45 Opening Exercises

Mrs. Allen reminds the children of the winter theme that will continue and uses the same pattern as for Monday and Tuesday to check the pan of water and record the weather. Mrs. Allen asks the children whether they have thought of what they will be painting on the winter mural they will begin today and calls the roll by asking what each one plans to add to the mural.

Mrs. Allen then reads a story about a fox searching for food in winter, *Red Fox Running* (Bunting, 1993). She helps the children identify of the elements of winter found in this story and leads a discussion of what happens to animals during winter in climates where it snows and gets very cold. She shows children a nonfiction book with photographs called *Winter Across America* (Simon, 1994) that is available in the class library. Again, she prompts the children to think about scenes of winter from these and other books they have read that might be good to include in the class mural [Tactical—Discussion] (*Science, Life Science—Animals*).

The class sings the "Dancing Snowflakes" song, then Mrs. Allen teaches them a new winter song, "The Snow Man," which ends with the children melting to the ground along with the words to the song [Tactical—Demonstrating] (*Music—Performing Music; Physical Education—Movement*). Together, they complete the opening exercise routines (calendar, days of the week, helpers chart). Mrs. Allen then explains that the children will be working with her at the big table during center time to get started on the mural. She also shows the group the large cardboard paper dolls and clothes sets that have been placed in the theme center, asking which clothes they will put on the dolls for winter and summer.

8:05 Large-Group Instruction

In large group, Mrs. Allen introduces the /r/ sound. She starts with a review of the letters they have been studying, then tells the children they will be learning the sound of the letter r so that they can pick out words that begin with the /r/ sound. She tells them that r spells the sound that starts rabbit, she demonstrates the /r/ sound and has them practice it with her. She shows them the letter r and tells them that this letter makes the /r/ sound, then she has them recite with her: "r, /r/, rabbit, r, /r/, rabbit" several times. She next provides several examples of words that start with the /r/ sound, emphasizing the initial (onset) sound (e.g., r . . . at, r . . . ed, r . . . ip, r . . . ob, r . . . un). As she says these words, she writes them on the board, pointing to the letters as she says the sounds. She then asks the children whether they can think of any words that start with the /r/ sound, and she writes these on the board and says them aloud in the same manner.

Next, she gives each child a card with a lowercase r written on it and instructs the children to close their eyes and listen to some words that start with the /r/ sound and some that don't. They are to hold up their cards when they hear words that start with r. As she presents each word, Mrs. Allen emphasizes being able to distinguish the beginning sound of r. She then passes out a worksheet with pictures of six objects, four of which start with the /r/ sound. She has the children circle the pictures that start with r, and she circulates among them, monitoring their efforts, giving feedback, and reteaching where needed [Direct Teaching] (*Language Arts, Reading—Letter-Sound Correspondence*). She tells them they will practice writing the letter r later in the day.

8:40 Special Areas (Parallel to Monday)
9:10 Center Time and Small-Group Instruction

As they get organized for center time, Mrs. Allen tells the children again that cutouts of children and clothing are available in the theme center (replaces snowflake activity) so they can dress the cutouts for winter. The playdough snowman activity is no longer available, and children are reminded that everyone needs to take time over the next two days to work with the teacher at the back table making a winter mural. She reminds them of the other options carried over from Monday and Tuesday, and calls four children to begin working on the mural.

A very large sheet of white butcher paper is spread across a large table near the sink, and brushes, water, and several watercolor sets have been prepared ahead of time. Mrs. Allen talks to children about what they plan to

Weather permitting, children need daily opportunities to play outside.

paint, where they will work on the mural, the approximate size they will make their pictures, and the colors and shapes they might use. She stays with the children and helps them monitor their decisions and actions as they paint [Tactical—Coaching] (*Art—Creating Art, Elements of Art*). She works with three or four children at a time on the mural, calling children to come when other students finish.

10:30 Clean-Up and Prepare for Lunch (Parallel to Monday)

10:40 Lunch (Parallel to Monday)

11:10 Outdoor Play Time (Parallel to Tuesday)

11:40 Quiet Story Time

For quiet story time, Mrs. Allen shows a video about wild animals in cold climates, *Alaska's Coolest Animals* (Zatz, 1997), and the class discusses how to care for pets during cold or snowy weather.

12:00 Large-Group Instruction

For this lesson, Mrs. Allen has sent home a note telling parents about the winter theme study and asked them to fill out a two-item questionnaire asking where they lived when they started school and if it snowed "a lot," "a little," or "not at all" during the winter there. She has collected the parent responses, and she has placed a map of North America on a corkboard where the children can see it clearly. She chose North America because she has two children whose parents were born in Mexico. She goes through the questionnaires, pointing out each place mentioned, talking about individual parents, and placing a colored push-pin on the map to indicate snowfall and mark locations (white for "a lot," blue for "a little," and yellow for "not at all"). Once she has marked the locations, Mrs. Allen asks the children to study how the pins are arranged, helping them to see the relationship between latitude and snowfall [Tactical—Discussion] (*Science, Earth and Space Science—Weather; Social Studies, Family—Family Histories*).

12:30 Center Time and Small-Group Instruction

The same centers are open this afternoon as this morning. Mrs. Allen has a parent volunteer who comes in on Wednesday afternoons, and this father directs the mural-painting activity (after Mrs. Allen explains the goals and procedures for the activity to him). Mrs. Allen calls five children at a time to work on writing the letter *r* with her at the back table. She has an *r* worksheet that prompts the children to trace *r*'s, complete partially printed *r*'s, then write *r*'s. Mrs. Allen models how to write the lower case *r*, reminds children of the /r/ sound, and helps children with their writing, depending on the level of support they need [Tactical—Modeling and Demonstrating; Incidental] (*Language Arts, Writing—Upper and Lowercase Letters*). Mrs. Allen rotates all of the children through this activity, calling new children to the table when those who write quickly have finished [Tactical—Grouping].

1:10 Clean-Up and Prepare to Dismiss (Parallel to Monday)

1:20 Closing Exercises

As the children review what they have learned, Mrs. Allen shows the map they made about where their parents lived when they were children, asks the children who worked on the mural to describe what they painted, and leads a quick review of the /r/ sound. She reminds them that they will continue the mural tomorrow and start planning the conclusion of their winter study for Friday.

1:30 Dismissal

Thursday

7:45 Opening Exercises

The same pattern is repeated today, both songs introduced this week are sung, and a new book, *Henrietta's First Winter* (Lewis, 1990), is read and discussed. Mrs. Allen and children reexamine the K-W-L chart they started on Monday and review what they have learned and are learning about winter. Mrs. Allen tells the children that they will be going to the computer lab today to learn more about animals that live in cold climates.

8:05 Large-Group Instruction

After the children gather at the tables for large-group instruction, Mrs. Allen tells them they will learn about dividing things in half today. She holds up cards showing several two-dimensional shapes, reviewing the names for each. She tells the children that if she draws a line so that each shape is separated into two equal parts, she has divided the shape in half. She then uses a straight edge to draw a heavy line on each shape, explaining each time that she is making two halves when she divides the shape into two equal parts. She also draws some lines that do not divide the shapes into equal parts and explains that these shapes are not divided in half. She then passes out graham crackers and explains that each cracker can be divided in half if it is broken on the line that runs down the middle. She demonstrates breaking the cracker carefully and has the children do the same. She then goes from child to child, asking them to quickly assess whether their crackers are divided in half or not (some will likely not break on the line). She then passes out a worksheet to be completed while the children eat their crackers. She circulates as children color one half of each shape on the sheet that is divided into equal halves, reinforcing those who have the concept and assisting those who do not [Direct Teaching] (*Math, Geometry—Geometric Shapers; Numbers and Operations—Fractions*).

8:40 Special Areas (Parallel to Monday)

9:10 Center Time and Small-Group Instruction

The doll cutout activity is available, as are the other centers from yesterday. Mrs. Allen reminds the children of their options, including a new activity at the water table. There, she has placed several ice pieces that have been frozen overnight in plastic tubs of various shapes and sizes. She shows the children the colored salt water and eyedroppers she has placed in the water table with the ice. She demonstrates how they are to drop the colored salt water onto the ice to see what effect it has. She tells them she has more ice for this afternoon, but that everyone should get to this center sometime today [Tactical—Modeling and Demonstrating] (*Science, Physical Science—Matter; Science Processes—Investigation*). Mrs. Allen announces that any children who have not finished their parts of the mural should join her now.

Mrs. Allen finishes up with the children who need to complete their mural parts, then she spends time at the water table interacting with children who are dropping salt water of various colors onto the ice. She supports those who may have trouble using the eyedroppers, and she asks questions that encourage children to predict what will happen, observe what is happening, try to explain what they are observing, and connect their activity to elements of the real world (e.g., spreading salt on roads and sidewalks after a snowstorm) [Incidental Teaching] (*Sciences Processes—Observation, Hypothesizing, Investigation, Interpretation, Communication*). Because Gina cannot reach into the water table, Mrs. Allen brings Gina to a low table next to the water table where she has

---

APPLICATIONS

Because Gina cannot reach into the water table, the teacher brings Gina to a low table next to the water table where she has prepared a separate tub.

Imagine that the first-grade teachers at your school are very anxious about having a student in a wheelchair in their classroom next year. They believe that the extra effort it takes to accommodate a student with special needs will take time and energy away from meeting the needs of the other children in the class. What would you say to these teachers? What could you do to help them deal with the conflicts of including children with disabilities in the full range of classroom activities?

prepared a separate tub with its own ice piece and colored salt water. Mrs. Allen asks Gina to invite another child to work with her, and the two children complete the activity in the separate tub [Tactical—Grouping].

10:30 Clean-Up and Prepare for Lunch (Parallel to Monday)
10:40 Lunch (Parallel to Monday)
11:10 Outdoor Play Time (Parallel to Tuesday)
11:40 Quiet Story Time

Mrs. Allen reads *My Horse of the North* (McMillan, 1997), a book with beautiful winter photographs of a girl and her horse in Iceland. Mrs. Allen shows the children where Iceland is on a world map and tells them they will be going to the computer lab for large-group instruction. There they will visit a Web site about animals that live in the arctic. She shows them where the arctic region is on the map, compares it to Iceland and the United States, and asks children to predict what kind of animals might live so far north.

12:00 Large-Group Instruction

The children assemble in the computer lab where they sit in pairs and are assisted by their teacher, the computer specialist, and two parents who serve as lab volunteers. The adults help the children go to a preselected Web site (e.g., www.EnchantedLearning.com/biomes/) where they find information about animals that live in arctic regions. With the computer specialist leading, the adults and children explore the kinds of animals that live in the arctic and discover the adaptations animals make to the cold, icy conditions. Each child downloads and prints an outline drawing of an arctic animal that he/she can color back in the classroom or at home [Tactical—Grouping; Coaching] (*Science, Life Science—Animals*; *Earth and Space Science—Weather*).

12:30 Center Time and Small-Group Instruction

Back in the classroom, the children are reminded that new ice has been placed in the water table and that those who didn't get to that center this morning should be sure to go there this afternoon. The same activities are available as this morning, and the children are prompted to color the arctic animal they just printed out in the computer lab if they wish. Mrs. Allen takes this opportunity to work one-

Carefully planned experiences with computers can provide opportunities for learning in many curriculum areas.

on-one with Dorene, Rod, and other children who need more help with the "one half" concept. She has set aside geometric shapes, a straightedge, and markers to work with these children and others who want to join her [Tactical—Tutoring].

1:10 Clean-Up and Prepare to Dismiss (Parallel to Monday)
1:20 Closing Exercises

Mrs. Allen leads the group in making a chart that sequences the events of the day. She asks what did we do first, next, and so on, leading them through the day. She starts with the numeral 1 and adds a numeral for each activity that is named in order. Once the chart is complete, she talks about sequence and emphasizes how much they are learning every day [Tactical—Discussion]

(*Language Arts, Listening—Comprehension*). She tells the children that tomorrow they will make ice cream to celebrate their theme study of winter.

1:30 Dismissal

Friday

7:45 Opening Exercises

The same pattern is followed for opening exercises. When the pan of water is checked and the chart is filled in, Mrs. Allen helps the children use the information in the chart to summarize what they have learned about temperature and freezing water. She tells them that after opening exercises they will do an activity to see how water can take three different forms. She lets the group select one of the winter books read this week to be read again this morning, and she leads the singing of the two songs they have learned this week. After calendar, days of the week, and helpers chart, individual children say words that begin with the /r/ sound as they are released to go to the back of the room for a science demonstration. Mrs. Allen provides lots of scaffolding in the form of hints and prompts for those who cannot think of new /r/ words.

8:05 Large-Group Instruction

In preparation for the demonstration, Mrs. Allen prepared a tray of ice cubes and brought in an electric kettle. She begins by showing the ice cubes and letting children touch them. She next asks the children to predict what will happen when she puts the ice cubes into the kettle and plugs it in. She then heats some of the ice cubes in the kettle. While the kettle is heating, she asks the children for descriptive words that tell how the ice cubes she has placed into a plastic bag look, feel, and sound, and she writes their words on a chart under "Ice." When the ice in the kettle has melted, she pours the warm water into a clear pitcher and leads a discussion of what happened to the ice. She helps the children see that water was frozen to make ice, then melted back into water. She has them study the way water looks in the pitcher and how it sounds as she pours it back into the kettle. Mrs. Allen now asks the children to predict what will happen when she now makes the water very hot. While the kettle comes to a boil, the teacher asks for words that describe how water looks, feels, and sounds, which she records on the chart under "Water." When the kettle begins hissing, she helps them see that water is changed to steam when it boils. She reminds them that hot water is dangerous, and points out that the steam coming from the kettle is another form of water called a gas. She leads as the children generate a list of descriptive words, which she writes under "Steam."

Mrs. Allen concludes by reviewing what the class has learned from the activity, going over the chart, and helping the children see that water can take three distinct forms [Tactical—Demonstration] (*Science, Physical Science—Matter; Science Processes—Observation, Hypothesizing, Investigation, Interpretation, Communication; Language Arts, Writing—Dictating Messages and Stories*). She tells the children that they will be turning a liquid into a solid this afternoon when they make ice cream to celebrate the conclusion of their winter theme study.

8:40 Special Areas (Parallel to Monday)
9:10 Center Time and Small-Group Instruction

Options are the same at centers today except that the water table ice activity is not available, and reading partners from the fifth grade are coming for 20 minutes

Reading partner programs can benefit both the kindergartners and the older children with whom they work.

The older children were trained early in the year and understand the teacher's goals that the younger children read as much as possible with the support of the fifth graders.

Imagine that you want to start a reading partners program so that upper-grade elementary students in your school can read with your kindergartners. Write out the steps that you will need to take in order to make this happen. Who will you have to contact? How will you recruit volunteers? What will be the criteria (if any) for upper-grade student participation? How will you train the older children? How will you set up a schedule? How will you prepare your kindergartners? What will you do when students are absent? What else will you need to consider?

to read with the children. Each child has been assigned to a fifth grader, and each Friday, Mrs. Allen provides selected books for the partners to share. The older children were trained early in the year and understand the teacher's goals that the younger children read as much as possible with the support of the fifth graders [Tactical—Tutoring] (*Language Arts, Reading—Simple Text Readings*).

10:30 Clean-Up and Prepare for Lunch (Parallel to Monday)
10:40 Lunch (Parallel to Monday)
11:10 Outdoor Play Time

Because it has snowed, this time is spent collecting snow in plastic buckets and placing them just outside the door in preparation for making ice cream during this afternoon's center time.

11:40 Quiet Story Time

This time is spent making captions to go with the class winter mural. Mrs. Allen has attached the mural to the wall and moves from one child's artistic contribution to the next, asking individual children to talk about what they painted, then writing dictation from each child to go with his/her portion of the mural. Mrs. Allen helps the children read back the words, phrases, and sentences that they dictate. She concludes by leading the children in an assessment of the learning that happened while they were planning, making, and writing captions for the mural [Tactical—Discussion] (*Language Arts, Reading—Correspondence Between Spoken and Written Words; Writing—Dictating Messages and Stories*).

12:00 Large-Group Instruction

Mrs. Allen divides the kindergartners into two-person teams to "read and write the room." She organizes teams so that more able readers and writers are paired with those who need more support, including Rod and Dorene. Each pair gets a pointer, clipboard, and pencil. The task is for each pair to find, read, and write six words displayed around the room. For the first three words, the child who starts with the pointer points to a word the team agrees on and spells the word while the one with the clipboard writes the word on the paper Mrs. Allen has prepared with six numbered lines. After three words are written, team members switch roles. The words are found on language experience charts, on labels Mrs. Allen has placed on objects and centers; on a word wall that includes sight words and other important words children are learning; on the children's cubbies; on environmental print; on books, games, and puzzles; on word family charts and other bulletin boards; and today on the winter mural. Mrs. Allen circulates, pointing out word options and supporting children's reading and writing. Once the children have written their six words, they sit in a circle on the carpet and take turns reading their words to the group [Tactical—Grouping] (*Language Arts, Reading—Environmental Print; Writing—Upper and Lowercase Letters, Conventional Spelling*).

12:30 Center Time and Small-Group Instruction

Mrs. Allen has invited two parent volunteers to help with ice cream making. She divides the children into three groups and assigns one adult (including herself) to each group. She tells the children that they will be making and eating ice cream as a way to celebrate all they have learned about winter this week. She describes the ingredients and materials that have been placed at the three tables. She goes over a recipe she has written on chart paper: 1 tablespoon sugar, 1/2 cup half-and-half, 1/4 teaspoon vanilla. With help from the parent volunteers, the children measure the ingredients into small zippered plastic bags and seal them tightly. Next, the adults place the snow gathered earlier or ice prepared ahead of time into large (gallon-sized) zippered bags until half full, then rock salt is added to the snow or ice. The small bag is then sealed inside the larger bag, and the children shake the bags gently until the mixture turns to ice cream. While the ice cream is turning from liquid to solid, the teacher reminds the children of the three forms of matter they discussed earlier and of the activity with the ice and salt water they did at the water table. After the mixture turns to ice cream (about five minutes), the adults help the children open the large bags and wipe off and open the small bags. The children add sprinkles and fruit if they choose and eat with a spoon.

1:10 Clean-Up and Prepare to Dismiss

The children and adults help clean up after the ice cream treat, and the children prepare to go home for the weekend.

1:20 Closing Exercises

Mrs. Allen leads the children through the L step in the K-W-L process, asking them to tell her what they have learned about winter during this week's activities. She records their answers on the chart and tells them that she will make a copy of their K-W-L chart and send it home in next week's newsletter so they can share with their parents all they learned about winter.

1:30 Dismissal

 APPLICATIONS

Every setting and every teacher is unique.

Imagine that you are starting a kindergarten teaching job in a setting that gives you a great deal of autonomy in how you set up and run your classroom. If you were given a virtually free hand in determining what would be taught, how it would be taught, and how the classroom and school day would be organized, what would you do? What are your professional beliefs about what counts in setting up a kindergarten program? How would you put your beliefs into action? Consider, on the other hand, what you would do if you worked at a school in which the kindergarten curriculum was "set in stone" and teaching strategies were prescribed by the district. How would this affect your views on what kindergarten should be like, and what would you do if your views conflicted with the expectations of your job?

Closing Thoughts

This chapter provides a concrete example of what a week might look like in a new kindergarten. But it is only an example. Every setting and every teacher will be different. In some settings, teachers will feel they don't have time to integrate instruction around a theme like winter. In others, teachers will place less emphasis on direct teaching than was evident in the example. In some settings, teachers will be running two half-day programs. In others, they will be teaching on the same full-day schedule as the rest of the elementary school. In some settings, most of the children will require the extra support Dorene and Rod needed in the example. In others, many of the children will be farther along in their development than children in the imaginary class. In some settings, the state or district curriculum will be more explicit and more demanding than the one presented here. In others, it may be hard to determine exactly what the kindergarten curriculum includes. These and other constraints mean that no classroom will look exactly like the one described. Real teachers will have to adjust to real settings. But if they are committed to the ideas behind the example, good teachers will be able to create their own version of a new kindergarten in virtually any setting.

As has been stressed throughout this book, teachers are the professionals who know best what constitutes best practice in the kindergartens where they work. But teachers need to adjust to a world that has changed and continues to change. Traditional approaches may need to be reexamined in the face of differences in the experience of childhood, the growing knowledge base in early childhood education, and the push of accountability in classrooms for our youngest learners. Teachers need a strong sense of what should be taught, a well-developed repertoire of teaching strategies, and a deliberate plan for ensuring that classrooms are places in which children learn a little every day. As I have argued, I believe moving to a more balanced approach to kindergarten teaching is needed, and I hope the elements described throughout this book and demonstrated in this chapter will help teachers create a balance that meets the complex needs of young children and satisfies the evolving expectations of the systems in which kindergartens are embedded—that is, teaching the child and meeting the standards. This is the essential challenge of teaching in the new kindergarten.

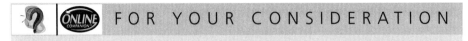

FOR YOUR CONSIDERATION

1. What elements of the new kindergarten distinguish it from developmental or academic approaches?

2. What factors support the shift to a new kindergarten, and what factors constrain such a shift?

3. Which characteristics of the new kindergarten would be difficult to explain and justify (to parents, administrators, other teachers), and which would be easy?

4. What are alternative approaches to addressing the conditions that impact contemporary kindergarten teaching?

5. What will kindergarten curriculum and teaching look like in ten years?

LEARNING ACTIVITIES

INDIVIDUAL ACTIVITIES

- Go through the week's plan in the chapter and identify activities that would need to be changed if the majority of the students in the class appeared to have the learning difficulties described for Rod and Dorene. Make an adjusted plan based on the needed changes.

- Using a kindergarten class with which you are familiar (or the one described in this chapter), create a week's plan that covers a week in October or March. Adjust the curriculum content to the time of year, and select an appropriate unit, theme, or project topic to build into your plan.

SMALL GROUP ACTIVITIES

- Collect and study recommended class schedules from state and district curriculum guides, professional publications, and real teachers. Then work together to construct a daily kindergarten schedule based on the beginning and ending times of a local school district.

- Bring in your favorite kindergarten picture book and share it with your group. Then, dividing by days of the week, work through the week's plan in the chapter, and make changes that would be needed if the week's integrated theme were not winter, but built around one of your group's children's books.

Continues

LEARNING ACTIVITIES *continued*

LARGE GROUP ACTIVITIES

- Lead a discussion exploring issues of teacher autonomy in relation to developing a new kindergarten in schools they know about. Think about and describe the status quo of kindergarten curriculum and teaching in local schools. Speculate on how well the new kindergarten approach recommended in this book would be received in those schools. Discuss ways to move individual classrooms in the direction of the new kindergarten, even in settings where change may not be encouraged.

- Set up a fishbowl role-playing activity, during which selected students pretend to be kindergarten teachers while others play the roles of parents. Give students time to prepare for their roles. "Teachers" should be prepared to explain what they do in their kindergarten and why they do it. "Parents" should be concerned about their children and not sure that the new kindergarten approach is what they want. Selected sets of students sit in the center of the group (the fishbowl) and role-play parent-teacher conferences. Following the role-play, the group discusses the form and substance of the conferences they participated in and/or observed.

References

AAAS. (2001). *Designs for science literacy.* Washington, DC: American Association for the Advancement of Science.

Becker, W. C., Engelmann, S., Carnine, D. W., & Rhine, W. R. (1981). Direct instruction model. In W. R. Rhine (Ed.), *Making schools more effective: New directions from Follow Through* (pp. 95–154). New York: Academic Press.

Bedrova, E., & Leong, D. J. (1996). *Tools of the mind: The Vygotskian approach to early childhood education.* Englewood Cliffs, NJ: Prentice-Hall.

Benner, S. M., & Barclay-McLaughlin, G. (2003). Simultaneous curricular reform in urban education and teacher preparation: A partnership approach. Unpublished paper, University of Tennessee, Knoxville.

Bereiter, C., & Engelmann, S. (1966). *Teaching disadvantaged children in the preschool.* Upper Saddle River, NJ: Prentice Hall.

Berk L. E., & Winsler, A. (1995). *Scaffolding children's learning: Vygotsky and early childhood education.* Washington, DC: National Association for the Education of Young Children.

Block, J. H. (Ed.). (1971). *Mastery learning: Theory and practice.* New York: Holt, Rinehart, and Winston.

Bloom, B. S. (1976). *Human characteristics and school learning.* New York: McGraw-Hill.

Bransford, J. D., Brown, A. L., & Cocking, R. R. (Eds.). (1999). *How people learn: Brain, mind, experience, and school.* Washington, DC: National Academy Press.

Bredekamp, S., & Copple, C. (Eds.). (1997). *Developmentally appropriate practice in early childhood programs.* Washington, DC: National Association for the Education of Young Children.

Brett, J. (1989). *The mitten.* New York: Putnam.

Bunting, E. (1993). *Red fox running.* New York: Clarion.

CNAEA. (1994). *National standards for arts education: What every young American should know and be able to do in the arts.* Reston, VA: Consortium of National Arts Education Associations.

Cadwell, L. B. (1997). *Bringing Reggio Emilia home: An innovative approach to early childhood education.* New York: Teachers College Press.

Cannella, G. S., & Bailey, C. (1999). Postmodern research in early childhood education. *Advances in Early Education and Care, 10,* 3–39.

Carnine, D., Carnine, L., Karp, J., & Weisberg, P. (1988). Kindergarten for economically disadvantaged children: The direct instruction component. In C. Warger (Ed.), *A resource guide to public school early childhood programs* (pp. 73–98). Alexandria, VA: Association for Supervision and Curriculum Development.

Carroll, J. B. (1971). Problems of measurement related to the concept of learning for mastery. In J. H. Block (Ed.), *Mastery learning: Theory and practice* (pp. 29–46). New York: Holt, Rinehart, and Winston.

Chen, J., Krechevsky, M., & Viens, J. (1998). *Building on children's strengths: The experience of Project Spectrum.* New York: Teachers College Press.

Cook, R. E., Tessier, A., & Klein, M. D. (2000). *Adapting early childhood curricula for children in inclusive settings.* Upper Saddle River, NJ: Prentice-Hall.

Davies, M. A. (2000). Learning . . . The beats goes on. *Childhood Education, 76,* 148–153.

Delton, J. (1982). *A walk on a snowy night.* New York: Harper & Row.

Department of Health and Human Services. (1996). *Physical activity and health: A report of the Surgeon General.* Atlanta, GA: Centers for Disease Control and Prevention.

Dever, M. T., Falconer, R. C., & Kessenich, C. (2003). Implementing developmentally appropriate practices in a developmentally inappropriate climate: Assessment in kindergarten. *Dimensions of Early Childhood, 31,* 27–33.

Edwards, C., Gandini, L., & Forman, G. (Eds.). (1993). *The hundred languages of children: The Reggio Emilia approach to early childhood education.* Norwood, NJ: Ablex.

Elkind, D. (1994). *Ties that stress: The new family imbalance.* Cambridge, MA: Harvard University Press.

Elkind, D. (2001). *The hurried child: Growing up too fast too soon.* Cambridge, MA: Perseus.

Feldman, D. H. (1994). *Beyond universals in cognitive development.* Norwood, NJ: Ablex.

Gardner, H. (1993). *Multiple intelligences: The theory in practice.* New York: Basic Books.

Gardner, H. (1998). Are there additional intelligences? In J. Kane (Ed.), *Education, information, and transformation* (pp. 111–131). Englewood Cliffs, NJ: Prentice Hall.

Goffin, S. G., & Wilson, C. S. (2001). *Curriculum models and early childhood education: Appraising the relationship.* Upper Saddle River, NJ: Merrill Prentice Hall.

Goffman, E. (1959). *The presentation of self in everyday life.* Garden City, NY: Anchor Books.

Goffman, E. (1967). *Interaction ritual: Essays on face-to-face behavior.* Chicago: Aldine.

Hatch, J. A. (1992). Improving language instruction in the primary grades: Strategies for teacher-controlled change. *Young Children, 47,* 54–60.

Hatch, J. A. (2000). Introducing postmodern thought in a thoroughly modern university. In L. D. Soto (Ed.), *The politics of early childhood education* (pp. 179–195). New York: Peter Lang.

Hatch, J. A. (2002). Accountability shovedown: Resisting the standards movement in early childhood education. *Phi Delta Kappan, 83,* 457–462.

Hatch, J. A., & Freeman, E. B. (1988). Kindergarten philosophies and practices: Perspectives of teachers, principals, and supervisors. *Early Childhood Research Quarterly, 3,* 151–166.

Hatch, J. A., & Grieshaber, S. (2002). Child observation and accountability: Perspectives from Australia and the United States. *Early Childhood Education Journal, 29,* 227–231.

Helm, J. H., & Katz, L. G. (2001). *Young investigators: The project approach in the early years.* New York: Teachers College Press.

Hoff, D. J. (2002). Measuring results. *Education Week, 21,* 48–52. (January 10, 2002).

IRA/NAEYC. (1998). *Learning to read and write: A joint position statement.* Washington, DC: International Reading Association and National Association for the Education of Young Children.

Jacobson, L. (2001, September 26). Experts say young children need more math. *Education Week*, p. 57.

Johnson, D. W., & Johnson, R. T. (1999). *Learning together and alone: Cooperative, competitive, and individualistic learning.* Boston: Allyn and Bacon.

Johnson, J. R. (1999). The forum on early childhood science, mathematics, and technology education. In *Dialogue on early childhood science, mathematics, and technology education* (pp. 14–25). Washington, DC: American Association for the Advancement of Science.

Joyce, B., Hrycauk M, & Calhoun, E. (2003). Learning to read in kindergarten: Has curriculum development bypassed the controversies? *Phi Delta Kappan, 85,* 126–132.

Judge, S. L., & Parette, H. P. (Eds.). (1998). *Assistive technology for young children with disabilities : A guide to family-centered services.* Cambridge, MA: Brookline Books.

Katz, L. G., & Chard, S. C. (1989). *Engaging children's minds: The project approach.* Norwood, NJ: Ablex.

Keats, E. J. (1962). *The snowy day.* New York: Viking Press.

Kilpatrick, J., Swafford, J., & Findell, B. (Eds.) (2001). *Adding it up: Helping children learn mathematics.* Washington, DC: National Academy Press.

Kretzmann, J. P., & McKnight, J. L. (1993). *Building communities from the inside out.* Evanston, IL: Asset-Based Community Development Institute Publications.

Lemlech, J. K. (2002). *Curriculum and instructional methods for the elementary and middle school.* Upper Saddle River, NJ: Merrill Prentice Hall.

Lewis, R. (1990). *Henrietta's first winter.* New York: Farrar, Straus, and Giroux.

McMillan, B. (1997). *My horse of the north.* New York: Scholastic.

NAEYC/NCTM. (2002). *Early childhood mathematics: Promoting good beginnings.* Washington, DC: National Association for the Education of Young Children & National Council for Teachers of Mathematics.

NASPE, (2000). *Appropriate practices in movement programs for young children ages 3–5.* Reston, VA: National Association for Sport and Physical Education.

National Reading Panel. (2000). *Report of the National Reading Panel: Teaching children to read.* Washington, DC: National Institute of Child Health and Human Development.

NCSS. (1994). *Curriculum standards for the social studies: Expectations of excellence.* Washington, DC: National Council for the Social Studies.

NCTM. (2000). *Principles and standards for school mathematics.* Reston, VA: National Council for Teachers of Mathematics.

NEA. (2000). *Ten proven principles for teaching reading.* Washington, DC: National Education Association.

NRC. (1996). *National science education standards.* Washington, DC: National Research Council.

Neuman, S. B., Copple, C., & Bredekamp, S. (2000). *Learning to read and write: Developmentally appropriate practices for young children.* Washington, DC: National Association for the Education of Young Children.

O'Brien, B. (1999). *Learning to read through the arts.* Glenn Rock, NJ: Learning to Read Through the Arts.

Phillips, M. B., & Hatch, J. A. (2000a). Why teach? Prospective teachers' reasons for entering the profession. *Journal of Early Childhood Teacher Education, 21,* 373–384.

Phillips, M. B., & Hatch, J. A. (2000b). Practicing what we preach in teacher education. *Dimensions in Early Childhood Education, 28,* 24–30.

Postman, N. (1982). *The disappearance of childhood.* New York: Delacorte.

Rand, M. K. (2000). *Giving it some thought: Cases for early childhood practice.* Washington, DC: National Association for the Education of Young Children.

Rogoff, B. (1990). *Apprenticeship of thinking: Cognitive development in social context.* New York: Oxford University Press.

Rosenshine, B., & Meister, C. (1994). Reciprocal teaching: A review of the research. *Review of Educational Research, 64,* 479–530.

Rosenshine, B. V., & Stevens, R. J. (1986). Teaching functions. In M. C. Wittrock (Ed.), *Third handbook of research on teaching* (pp. 376–391). New York: Macmillan.

Schickedanz, J. A. (1999). *Much more than ABCs: The early stages of reading and writing.* Washington, DC: National Association for the Education of Young Children.

Simon, S. (1994). *Winter across America.* New York: Hyperion.

Slavin, R. E. (1995). *Cooperative learning: Theory, research, and practice.* Boston: Allyn and Bacon.

Slavin, R. E. (1997). *Educational psychology: Theory and practice.* Boston: Allyn and Bacon.

Snow, C. E., Burns, M. S., & Griffin, P. (1998). *Preventing reading difficulties in young children.* Washington, DC: National Academy Press.

Stanulis, R. N., & Manning, B. H. (2003). *K–8 classroom methods: From teacher reflection to student responsibility.* Upper Saddle River, NJ: Merrill Prentice Hall.

Torgan, C. (2002). Childhood obesity on the rise. *NIH Word on Health, June,* 1–4.

Vygotsky, L. S. (1962). *Thought and language.* Cambridge, MA: MIT Press. (Original work published in 1934).

Vygotsky, L. S. (1978). *Mind and society: The development of higher mental processes.* Cambridge, MA: Harvard University Press. (Original work published in 1930).

Vygotsky, L. S. (1993). *The collected works of L. S. Vygotsky: The fundamentals of defectology.* R. W. Rieber & A. S. Carton (Eds.). New York: Plenum.

Washington, V., & Andrews, J. D. (Eds.). (1998). *Children of 2010.* Washington, DC: Children of 2010.

Wassermann, S. (1993). *Getting down to cases: Learning to teach with case studies.* New York: Teachers College Press.

Wertsch, J. V. (1991). *Voices of the mind: A sociocultural approach to mediated action.* Cambridge, MA: Harvard University Press.

Wolery, M., & Wilbers, J. S. (1994). *Including Children with Special Needs in Early Childhood Programs.* Washington, DC: National Association for the Education of Young Children.

Zatz, D. (1997). *Alaska's coolest animals* (videotape). Anchorage, AK: SkyRiver Films.

Index

Note:

The letter "b" following a page number represents boxed material

The letter "f" following a page number represents a figure

The letter "t" following a page number represents a table

AAAS. *See* American Association for the Advancement of Science (AAAS)

Abilities
balancing differences in, 132–138
cognitive impairments and, 137–138
emotional and behavioral impairments and, 136–137
hearing impairments and, 134
physical impairments and, 135
visual impairments and, 134–135

Accountability shovedown, 16–18

Action, short and long-term, 147–149

Activities
balancing the presentation of, 120–123
classroom schedule and, 121–123
learning *vs.* fun and, 120b, 121

Addition, concept of, 39f, 41

ADHD. *See* Attention deficit hyperactivity disorder (ADHD)

Algebra, 43
comparing and ordering in, 43, 102
in mathematics curriculum, 39f, 43
number sentences in, 41, 43
patterns in, 43

Alphabetic principle, 30f, 31

American Association for the Advancement of Science (AAAS), science and, 46

Animals, in life science curriculum, 47f, 48

Arrangement
classroom spatial, 116–117
of space, 116–119

Art and music
creating art, 63, 63f, 106
culture and music, 65
curriculum outline, 63f
deriving meaning from art, 63f, 64, 106
deriving meaning from music, 63f, 65, 106
direct teaching for, 107
elements of art, 63–64, 63f, 107
elements of music, 63f, 65
incidental teaching for, 106
overview, 62–65
performing music, 63f, 64
tactical teaching for, 106
thematic teaching for, 106

Assessment
balancing, 129–132
documentation and, 131–132, 131b
dynamic, 130–131
of teaching in classroom, 130

Attention deficit hyperactivity disorder (ADHD), 136, 145

Balanced approach, teaching and, 8–9, 15

Balancing
the arrangement of space, 116–119
assessment, 129–132
differences in children's abilities, 132–138
and keeping classroom equilibrium, 142–149
the organization of time, 124–129
parent and community involvement, 138–142
rights and responsibilities, 113–116
teaching strategies, 121–123

Behaviorism, 14
Behaviorists, 8, 10, 15
Bereiter-Engelmann model, 96
Body. *See* The human body
Body awareness
    in physical education curriculum, 58f
    using incidental teaching for, 105
Brainstorming, 146–147
British Infant School, project approach
    in, 82

Center time and small group instruction
    on Friday schedule, 173–174, 175–176
    on Monday schedule, 156–157
    on sample schedule, 124f
    on Thursday schedule, 169–170
    on Tuesday schedule, 161–162, 163
    on typical schedule, 126, 127–128
    on Wednesday schedule, 165–166,
        167
Change
    children and, 7
    growth and, 52f, 53–54, 104
Children
    change and, 7
    as collaborators, 11
    as communicators, 11
    content of media and, 5–6
    hurried, 7
    influence of media on, 5
    learning and postmodern values, 6–7
    out-of-home care, 4, 7
    and political forces, 16–18
    as protagonists, 11
Classification, in science processes, 50
Classroom
    assessment of teaching in, 130
    guidelines for organization of, 117–119
    learning centers and, 119
    management, 111
    one week instruction example,
        152–176
    restoring balance in, 143, 143b
    rules, 114–115, 115b
    schedule, 121–123
    as shared space, 119
    spatial arrangements, 116–117

Clean-up and prepare for lunch
    on sample schedule, 124f
    on typical schedule, 126
    on one week schedule, 157, 162, 166,
        170, 174
Clean-up and prepare to dismiss
    on one week schedule, 159, 163, 167,
        171, 176
    on sample schedule, 124f
    on typical schedule, 128
Clean-up and small-group instruction,
    124f, 126
Closing exercises
    on one week schedule, 159, 163–164,
        167–168, 171–172, 176
    on sample schedule, 124f
    on typical schedule, 128
CNAEA. *See* Consortium of National
    Arts Education Associations
    (CNAEA)
Coaching, 88–89, 105, 136–137
Cognitive impairments, 137–138
Collaborators, children as, 11
Communication
    active two-way, 142
    in science processes, 51
Communicators, children as, 11
Community
    consumption and, 52f, 56–57,
        104–105
    distribution and, 52f, 56–57, 104–105
    involvement, balancing parent and,
        138–142
    kinds of work and, 52f, 57
    production and, 52f, 56–57, 104–105
    rights and responsibilities in, 52f, 56
    rules and laws, 52f, 56, 104
    school settings and leaders of, 139b
    in social studies curriculum, 52f,
        56–57
    values, traditions and customs, 52f,
        57
Community mapping, 141
Community of learners, 112–113
Comparing
    counting skills, 43
    data analysis, 46

in kindergarten, 37
self and others, 53
Comparing and ordering
in algebra, 43, 102
using tactical teaching for, 102
Comprehension
listening, 30f, 37
reading, 30f, 33, 33b
Concept of number, 39f, 40
Consortium of National Arts Education
Associations (CNAEA), 62
Constructivism, 14
Constructivists, 8, 10, 15
Consumption, community and, 52f,
56–57, 104–105
Content *versus* process, 26
A Continuum of teaching strategies,
74–99, 74f
direct teaching, 74f, 84–95
in art and music, 107
in language arts, 100
in mathematics, 102
in science, 103
in social studies, 104–105
incidental teaching, 74–76, 74f
in art and music, 106
in language arts, 100
in mathematics, 101–102
in science, 102–103
in social studies, 104
tactical teaching, 74f, 84–95
in art and music, 106
in language arts, 100
in mathematics, 102
in science, 103
in social studies, 104
thematic teaching, 74f, 79–84
in art and music, 106
in language art, 100
in mathematics, 102
in science, 103
in social studies, 104
Conventional spelling, 35–36
Conventions, writing, 35
Cooperative grouping, 86–87
Counting skills, 39f, 40, 43
Craftwork activities, 63

Creative art, 26
Culture
childhood and, 4
music and, 65
Curriculum, 25
implementing, 28
outline
for art and music, 63f
for health and physical education, 58f
for language arts, 30f
for mathematics, 39f
for science, 47f
for social studies, 52f
subject matter in, 26
Customs, community and, 52f, 57

Data analysis, 45–46
in mathematics curriculum, 39f
graphs, 45–46
tallies, 45
Decoding, 30f, 32
Demographic predictions, 17
Descriptive language, 30f, 37
Descriptive words, 160
*Developmentally Appropriate Practices in
Early Childhood Programs* (DAP)
(Bredekamp and Copple), 71
Developmentally delayed. *See* Cognitive
impairments
Directions, 30f, 37–38
Direct teaching
in art and music, 107
for cognitively impaired children,
137
in continuum of teaching strategies,
74f, 96–99
for emotionally and behaviorally
impaired children, 137
in health and physical education,
105–106
in language arts, 100–101
in mathematics, 102
overview, 96–99
in science, 103
in social studies, 104–105
steps of, 96–99
Disabilities. *See* Impairments

Discussion, 90–93
   guided, 90
   open-ended, 90–91
   questioning, 92–93
   semi-structured, 91–92
Dismissal
   on one week schedule, 159, 164, 168, 176
   on sample schedule, 124f
   on typical schedule, 128
DISTAR, 96
Distribution, community and, 52f, 56–57, 104–105
Documentation, balancing assessment and, 131–132, 131b
Drill-and-kill methods, 93
Dynamic assessment, 130–131

Early childhood
   Lev Vygotsky on, 9–10
   Reggio Emilia on, 10–11
   strengths of education in, 19
Earth and space science, 49
   in science curriculum, 47f
Education
   in early childhood, strengths of, 19
   kindergarten, in the twentieth century, 8–9
Elkind, David, 5, 7
Emilia, Reggio
   on creating art, 106
   on early childhood practice, 10–11
   project approach, 82
Emotional and behavioral impairments, 136–137
Environmental print, 30f, 31
Exercises
   closing, 124f, 128
   opening, 124f, 125
Expectations, changing, 16–18
Experiences, changing, 4–8

Family
   histories, 52f, 55
   nuclear, 5
   permeable, 5

   roles and responsibilities in, 52f, 55–56, 79
   similarities and differences in, 52f, 55
   in social studies curriculum, 55–56
   and teacher relationships, 138
Feelings, examination of, 52f, 55
Fine-and large motor skills, 105
First and last name, writing, 30f, 34
Fitness, in physical education curriculum, 58f, 61–62
Fractions, 39f, 42
Fun, learning vs., 120b, 121

Geometry, 43–44
   in mathematics curriculum, 39f
   spatial relationships in, 44
   teaching shapes in, 43–44
Government-subsidized preschool programs, 5
Grammatical construction, 30f, 37
Grand narratives, 14
Graphs, 45–46
Grouping, 85–87
Growth and change, 52f, 53, 104
Guided discussions, 90

Hands-on approaches, 93
Health and physical education
   body awareness and physical education, 60
   curriculum outline, 58f
   direct teaching for, 105–106
   fitness and physical education, 61–62
   incidental teaching for, 105
   movement and physical education, 60–61
   nutrition and health, 58f, 59, 105
   overview, 57–62
   personal habits and health, 58–59, 58f
   safety and health, 58f, 60, 105
   tactical teaching for, 105
   thematic teaching for, 105
Hearing impairments, 134
Heat, in physical science curriculum, 47f, 49
High-frequency words. See Word(s), sight

How People Learn (Bransford, Brown, and Cocking), 12, 76
The human body
    in life science curriculum, 47f, 48
    using direct teaching for, 103
Hurried children, 7
Hypothsizing, in science processes, 50

IEPs. *See* Individualized education programs (IEPs)
Impairments
    cognitive, 137–138
    emotional and behavioral, 136–137
    hearing, 134
    physical, 135
    visual, 134–135
Incidental teaching
    in art and music, 106
    in continuum of teaching strategies, 74–76, 74f
    in health and physical education, 105
    in language arts, 100
    in mathematics, 101–102
    overview, 74–76
    in science, 102–103
    in social studies, 104
Inclusive Early Childhood Education Program, 133
Individualization, 94–95
Individualized education programs (IEPs), 137–138
Individualizing instruction, 94
Instruction
    direct teaching and, 99
    large-group, 124f, 125–126, 127
    practice and, 93–94
    small-group, 124f, 127
Integrated theme studies, 79, 82–84
Intentional learning, 12
Interactive journals, 142
Internet. *See* Media
Interpretation, in science processes, 51
Intersubjectivity, 76, 77
Intervention ideas, 147
Invented spelling, 35
Investigation, in science processes, 50–51

Kindergarten
    comprehension skills in, 37
    education
        in the twentieth century, 8–9
    functions of, 25–26
    objectives and standards in, 28
    programs
        examining circumstances for creating, 15b
        subject matter in, 26
Knowledge
    of children and media, 6
    reading research syntheses as source of, 13
    Vygotsky and, 10
K-W-L chart, 91, 92, 153, 154

Land, in earth and space science curriculum, 47f, 49
Language, descriptive, 30f, 37
Language arts
    curriculum outline, 30f
    direct teaching for, 100–101
    incidental teaching for, 100
    listening as, 30f, 37–38
    overview, 29–30
    reading as, 30–34, 30f
    speaking as, 30f, 36–37
    tactical teaching for, 100
    thematic teaching for, 100
    writing as, 30f, 34–36
Large-group instruction
    on Friday schedule, 172–173, 175
    on Monday schedule, 154–155, 158
    on sample schedule, 124f
    on Thursday schedule, 170–171
    on Tuesday schedule, 160–161, 163
    on typical schedule, 125–126
    on Wednesday schedule, 165, 167
Learning
    assessment of, 130
    coaching and, 88–89
    intentional, 12
    as purpose, 111
    vs. fun, 120, 120b
Learning centers, classroom and, 119

Learning processes
    balancing differences in children's abilities and, 132–138
    balancing process and content, 26–27, 27b
    intentional learning and, 12b
Letters of alphabet, recognizing, 30f, 31
Letter-sound correspondence, 30f, 32, 100
    using direct teaching for, 100–101
Life science, 49
Light, in physical science curriculum, 47f, 49
Linear measurement, 45
Lists, producing, 91, 92
Listening
    in language arts curriculum outline
        attending to oral readings, 30f, 38
        comprehension, 30f, 37
        directions, 30f, 37–38
        vocabulary, 30f, 37
Lunch, in sample schedule, 124f, 126, 157, 162, 166, 170, 174
Mastery learning, 94
Mathematics
    curriculum outline, 39f
    direct teaching for, 102
    incidental teaching for, 101–102
    overview, 38–40
    tactical teaching for, 102
    thematic teaching for, 102
Matter, in physical science curriculum, 47f, 48
Maturationism, 14
Maturationists, 8
Measurement
    concepts, 45
    in mathematics curriculum, 39f
    money and time concepts and, 45
    non-standard, 45, 102
    overview, 44–45
Media
    children and content of, 5–6
    influence on children, 5
    knowledge of children and, 6

Modeling and demonstrating, 87–88, 102, 105, 106, 136–137
Modern *vs.* postmodern values, 6–7
Modified, full-day kindergarten, 125
Money and time concepts, measurement and, 45
Monitoring and adjusting, 98, 98b, 102, 106
Movement
    in physical education curriculum, 58f
    using tactical teaching for, 105
Movies. *See* Media
Multiple impairments, 135
Multiple intelligences, theory of, 11–12
Multiple truths, 14
Music. *See* Art and music

NAEYC. *See* National Association for the Education of Young Children (NAEYC)
National Association for the Education of Young Children and the National Council for the Teachers of Mathematics, 2000 (NAEYC/NCTM), 39
National Association for the Education of Young Children (NAEYC), 71, 138
National Council for Teachers of Mathematics (NCTM), 39–40
National Council for the Social Studies (NCSS), definition of social studies, 51
National Research Council (NRC)
    How People Learn (Bransford, Brown, and Cocking), 12, 76
    Mathematics Learning Study Committee, 38
    science and, 46
National Science Education Standards, 46
NCSS. *See* National Council for the Social Studies (NCSS)
NCTM. *See* National Council for Teachers of Mathematics (NCTM)
Needs
    meeting children's, 17
    vs. wants, 52f, 54
Newsletter, communication and, 141–142

Non-standard measurement, 45
  using thematic teaching for, 102
Nonuniversal theory, 11–12
NRC. *See* National Research Council
  (NRC)
Nuclear families, 5
Number and operations
  concept of addition in, 39f, 41
  concept of number in, 39f, 40
  concept of subtraction in, 39f, 41–42
  counting skills in, 39f, 40
  in mathematics curriculum, 39f
  fractions in, 39f, 42
  numerals in, 39f, 40–41, 101–102
  ordinal numbers in, 39f, 42, 102
  story problems in, 39f, 42
Number sentences, 41, 43
Number words, 39f, 41
Numerals, 39f, 40–41
  using incidental teaching for, 101–102
Nutrition
  in health curriculum, 58f
  using thematic teaching for, 105

Objectives and standards, kindergarten
  and, 28, 28b
Observation
  incidental teaching and, 102–103
  in science processes, 50
Open-ended discussions, 90–91
Opening exercises
  on Friday schedule, 172
  on Monday schedule, 153–154
  on sample schedule, 124f
  on Thursday schedule, 168
  on Tuesday schedule, 159–160
  on typical schedule, 125
  on Wednesday schedule, 164
Ordering, in algebra, 43
Ordinal numbers, 39f, 42
  using direct teaching for, 102
Organization, guidelines for classroom,
  117–119
Outdoor playtime
  on Friday schedule, 174
  on Monday schedule, 157–158
  on sample schedule, 124f

  on Thursday schedule, 170
  on Tuesday schedule, 162, 162b
  on typical schedule, 126–127
  on Wednesday schedule, 166
Out-of-home care, children and, 4, 7

Parent and community involvement, bal-
  ancing, 138–142
Parents, in school settings, 139b
Patterns, in Algebra, 43
Performing music, 63f, 64
Permeable families, 5
Personal health habits, in health curricu-
  lum, 58f
Phonemic awareness, 30, 30f
Physical education
  curriculum outline, 58f
  overview, 26, 60–62
  teaching body awareness in, 58f, 60,
  105
  teaching fitness in, 58f, 61–62
  teaching movement in, 58f, 60–61,
  105
Physical impairments, 135
Physical science, 48–49
  in science curriculum, 47f
Place, childhood and, 4
Plants
  in life science curriculum, 47f, 48
  using thematic teaching for, 103
Political forces, childhood and, 16–18
Postman, Neil, 5
Postmodern critique, discipline of, 14
Postmodern permeable families, 5
Postmodern values, learning of children
  and, 6–7
Practicing, 93–94
Prediction, kindergarten and, 37
Preschool programs. *See also* Curricu-
  lum; Schedule
  adjustment of, children's needs and,
  17b
  project spectrum in, 11–12
Preschool settings, experiences and, 5
Presenting new material, 95, 102, 103
Print conventions, reading, 30f, 31
Problem solving, teachers and, 70–74

Problem solving model, 71, 143–149
Production, community and, 52f, 56–57, 104–105
Projects, 79, 80–82
Project spectrum, 11–12
Protagonists, children as, 11
Providing independent practice, 98

Questioning, 92–93
Quiet story time
    on Friday schedule, 174–175
    on Monday schedule, 158
    on sample schedule, 124f
    on Thursday schedule, 170
    on Tuesday schedule, 162
    on typical schedule, 127
    on Wednesday schedule, 166

Reading
    daily, 13
    in language arts curriculum, 30f
        alphabetic principle, 30f, 31
        correspondence between spoken and written words, 30f, 31
        decoding, 30f, 32
        environmental print, 30f, 31
        letters of the alphabet, 30f, 31
        letter sound correspondence, 30f, 31–32, 100
        phonemic awareness, 30, 30f
        print conventions, 30f, 31
        rhymes, 30f, 32
        shared, 38
        sight words, 30f, 32
        vocabulary, 30f, 32–33
        word families, 30f, 32
Reading research syntheses, 13
Reciprocal relationships, 138–142
Reciprocity, 142
Responsibilities
    balancing rights and, 113–116
    and rights, in community, 52f, 56
    and roles , in family, 52f, 55–56, 79
Rhymes, identifying, 30f, 32
Rights and responsibilities
    balancing, 113–116
    family and, 52f, 55–56

Roles and responsibilities, family and, 52f, 55–56, 79
Routines, 128
Rules and laws
    community and, 52f, 56, 104
    using tactical teaching for, 104

Safety
    in health curriculum, 58f
    using direct method for teaching, 105
Scaffolding, 75, 76–78, 100
Schedule. *See also* Curriculum; Preschool programs
    importance of, 128–129
    sample of, 124f
    school, 121–123
    typical, 125–128
Science
    curriculum outline, 47f
    incidental teaching for, 102–103
    overview, 46–48
    teaching, 47b
Science content
    of earth and space science, 49
    of life science, 48
    of physical science, 48–49
Science processes
    classification, 50
    in science curriculum, 47f
    hypothesizing, 47f, 50
    interpretation of, 47f, 51
    investigation in, 47f, 50–51
    observation in, 47f, 50, 102–103
    overview, 49–50
Self
    characteristics of, 52–53, 52f
    growth and change, 52f, 53–54, 104
    needs *vs.* wants, 52f, 54
    and others, valuing of, 52f, 53
    in social studies curriculum, 52f
    using incidental teaching for, 104
Self-regulation, promoting, 78
Semi-structured discussions, 91–92
Sentence patterns, 30f, 37
Set the stage for learning, 97, 105–106

Shapes
  in art, 107
  in geometry, 43–44
Shared reading, 38
Sight words, 30f, 35
Simple text readings, 30f, 33–34
Sky, in earth and space science curricu-
    lum, 47f, 49
Social studies
  community in, 56–57
  curriculum outline, 52f, 56–57
  direct teaching for, 104–105
  family in, 55–56
  incidental teaching for, 104
  overview, 26, 51–52, 51–57
  self in, 52–55, 104
  tactical teaching for, 104
  thematic teaching for, 104
Sound, in physical science curriculum,
    47f, 49
Space
  balancing the arrangement of,
      116–119
    classroom as shared space, 119
    classroom spatial arrangements,
      116–117
    learning center, 119
    organizing space, 117–119
Spatial arrangements, of classroom,
    116–117
Spatial relationships, in geometry,
    44
Speaking
  in language arts curriculum
    descriptive language, 30f, 37
    grammatical construction, 30f, 36
    sentence patterns, 30f, 37
    story retelling, 30f, 36
    vocabulary, 30f, 36
Special areas
  on one week schedule, 155, 161, 165,
      169, 173
  on sample schedule, 124, 124f
  on typical schedule, 126
Spelling
  conventional, 35–36
  invented, 35

Standards and objectives, kindergarten
    and, 28, 28b
Standards-based reform, 16, 17
Story problems, 39f, 42
Story retelling, 30f, 36
Strategies
  balancing teaching activities, 121–123
  management, 114
Subtraction, concept of, 39f, 41–42
Systematic instruction, learning difficul-
    ties and, 13b

Tactical teaching
  in art and music, 106
  coaching and, 88–89
  in continuum of teaching strategies,
      74f
  direct teaching and, 96–99
  discussing, 90–93
  grouping, 85–87
  individualizing, 94–95
  in language arts, 100
  modeling and demonstrating, 87–88,
      102, 106
  overview, 84–95
  practicing, 93–94
  in social studies, 104
  tutoring and, 89–90, 100
Take-home packets, 142
Tallies, 45
Teacher(s)
  adjusting programs to meet children's
      needs, 17b
  children, family life and, 5
  grouping kindergartners and, 85–87
  as professional problem solver, 70–74
  questions of children, 92b
  role in encouraging reciprocal relation-
      ships, 140–141
  as seen by behaviorist, 10
  as seen by constructivists, 10
Thematic teaching
  in art and music, 106
  in continuum of teaching strategies,
      74f
  in health and physical education,
      105

integrated theme studies, 79, 82–84
   in language arts, 100
   in mathematics, 102
   overview, 79–84
   projects, 79, 80–82
   in science, 103
   in social studies, 104
   units, 79, 80
Theory of multiple intelligences, 11–12
Time
   balancing the organization of, 124–129
   childhood and, 4
   and money concepts, 45
Traditions, community and, 52f, 57
Transitions, 128–129
Tutoring, 89–90, 100
Twentieth century, history of kindergarten education in, 8–9
Two-way communication, active, 142

Understandings, changing, 8–15
Units, 79, 80
Upper-and lowercase letters
   using tactical teaching for, 100
   writing, 30F, 34

Valuation, of self and others, 52f, 53
Values, community and, 52f, 57
Video games. *See* Media
Visual impairments, 134–135
Vocabulary
   listening and, 30f, 37
   reading and, 30f, 32–33
   speaking and, 30f, 36
   teaching, 13
Vocabulary development, 30f, 36
Vygotsky, Lev
   on children's disability and development, 138
   on dynamic assessment, 130–131
   on early childhood, 9–10, 36
   on language and learning to think, 36
   on zone of proximal development, 75

Water, in earth and space science curriculum, 47f, 49
Weather
   in earth and space science curriculum, 47f, 49
   in the opening exercise, 154, 160
   using tactical teaching for, 103
Webs, producing, 91, 92
Word families, 30f, 32
Word(s)
   correspondence between spoken and written, 30f, 31
   descriptive, 160
   number, 39f, 41
   sight, 30f, 32, 35
Work, community and, 52f, 57
Worksheet-driven practice, 93–94
Writing
   in language arts curriculum
      conventional spelling, 30f, 35–36
      conventions, 30f, 35
      dictated messages and stories, 30f, 35
      first and last name, 30f, 34
      invented spelling, 30f, 35
      in language arts curriculum outline, 30f
      sight words, 30f, 35
      upper-and lowercase letters, 30f, 34, 100

Zone of proximal development (ZPD), 75